CYCLIST'S
TRAINING
DIARY

Vitesse Press
Brattleboro, Vermont

The purpose of this diary is to help you get the most from your cycling and to better understand how your habits and training affect your riding. The information you record can serve as a guide for future training.

We welcome your comments and suggestions about this *Cyclist's Training Diary*. After you have used it, if you have ideas about how the content or the format could be made even more helpful in future editions, please send your comments to: Training Diary, Vitesse Press, 28 Birge Street, Brattleboro, VT 05301-3206.

Front cover: Karen Kurreck in the 1993 Vuelta de Bisbee.
Quotes for this training diary were taken from the book, *Tales from the Bike Shop*, by Maynard Hershon. For a copy, send $16.95 (includes postage and handling) to Vitesse Press at the address below.

All photos, including cover, by Jim Safford of Photosport International.

ISBN 0-941950-32-8
Seventh revised edition, February 1994
Copyright © 1994 by Vitesse Press
Photos copyright © 1990-93 by Photosport International

Published by Vitesse Press
28 Birge Street, Brattleboro, VT 05301-3206

Designed by Optima Design Associates, Inc.
Manufactured in the U.S.A.

This may be one of the most helpful and informative books you'll ever own. But you have to write it yourself and it will only be as good as what you put into it.

Whether you are dedicated to achieving new levels of fitness in your recreational riding or to improving your results in competition, keeping a training diary is essential. Are you getting better? If you're not, why not? If you are, what made the difference and is there room for even more improvement?

Without facts about your past you can't plan for the future. Perhaps you did a six-week program of intervals. Unless you can gauge what kind of improvement you got from all that sweat and heavy breathing, you won't know whether to retain the regimen or modify it or forget it. In the same way you must be able to assess the benefits of a winter's weight training program to decide whether it is worth repeating during the next off-season.

Long-range planning for your training is nearly impossible without detailed record-keeping that can remind you exactly what you did during a certain day, week, or month and allow you to make judgments about its worth. The best way to be sure that such information is at hand when you need it is to keep a cycling diary.

The biggest benefits of keeping a diary don't come in the first year but in the years after, because of the comparisons you can make. If you keep a record of your workouts from year to year, you can see the results of different training methods, dietary changes, and equipment modifications.

One of the most basic things to record is your mileage — the total for the year and for any period within it. Notice the preseason build-up from January to March, for instance. Compare this to your racing performances as the season wears on. You might find that more preseason miles would give you the aerobic base to ride the early races more competitively while still retaining enthusiasm for later in the summer. In this book you can note your mileage each week, each month, and the total for the year to date. During the season, entries can reveal the change in racing performance due to high-intensity work like intervals or motorpacing. It is important to know how many weeks it takes to reach your peak through a given training regimen — say anaerobic sessions twice a week — so you can hit your top performance level for specific events.

For example, by looking back over a period of several years you might see how doing intervals once a week brings you along slowly to a peak in about 12 weeks while a schedule of three interval sessions per week gets you there in about half the time. With a solid aerobic base and this information, you know exactly how long it will take to reach top form. But this can be calculated only if you've kept a record of past training and racing performances.

If you do a winter weight program, careful entries will let you know from one year to the next how many sets, reps, and how much poundage you have used for each exercise. Comparing yearly race results helps you assess the value of specific exercises, as well as the relative benefits of different weight routines, such as circuit training versus a power program.

Training diaries are also a great place to record your race results. Put in the name of the event and the starting time, the weather, the category you rode, your placing and time, along with the names of those who finished ahead and behind. In this way you can compare your accomplishments in the same race from year to year and also see if you are improving or regressing in relation to others. You think you will remember results forever as you relive the competition after the event, but over the years the races will tend to run together in your mind. The diary never forgets.

Diaries let you analyze peaks and valleys in performance. You can do this through evaluation of race results or with periodic time trials. Once you have ridden either a personal record or a personal disaster you can look back at the preceding weeks and months to find out why it happened. In the case of great rides or a series of races in which you were consistently in top form, you can reproduce that preparation later.

Another valuable reason for keeping records is that you can track down the causes of injuries more easily. If you are having knee problems, an analysis of the diary may give you some clues. Did you change your shoes, cleat position, or saddle height last month? How about that long ride two weeks ago? Maybe it irritated ligaments and you haven't recovered because, as the diary shows, you got inspired and rode 300 miles in the next six days with one race and two interval sessions.

One thing diaries brutally reveal is the way we tend to get excited and overdo our training just when we are rounding into top form. Diaries mirror our ego, our stupidity and our unwillingness to accept our limits.

Body weight fluctuations over a year or a career can also be charted. You can find if you really do climb better when you are lighter or if you lose strength after your weight drops below a certain level.

A diary allows you to see the effect that time of day has on training. If you have to ride for three months from 5:30 to 7:30 a.m. due to a change in your work or school schedule, you can compare the results of that routine to the afternoon workouts you might be more accustomed to.

Riders can present all sorts of reasons and excuses for not keeping a diary, even though they know it could help their cycling. Some can't remember to make daily entries. This problem can be conquered by keeping the diary next to your bed and filling it in before going to sleep. Or a diary can be kept near the bike and data recorded when returning from each day's training ride.

There are some pitfalls of diary keeping, a main one being the recording of too much data and getting lost in trivial detail. You don't need graphs of daily caloric intake, a complete biorhythm chart, three pulse and blood pressure readings per day or a four-page narrative account of your mental processes during the ride. Just stick to a few important items.

Another danger some riders have encountered is the "diary miles syndrome." It is easy to get trapped in the belief that more miles equal better performance, the result being a constant struggle to make this week's total more than last week's which was more than the week before that, and so on. For a while there is great satisfaction in the mere recording of the ever-larger totals, but the time will surely come when the physical and mental strain causes a breakdown. Don't let the diary become an end in itself; make it an aid, not a tyrant.

Listed on each page are some suggestions for entries. Although it looks like it will take you longer to write down the information than it took to do the workout, all these notations can be made in about three minutes a day. Don't feel that you have to complete each item every day, or even at all. We've tried to include everything that anyone could possibly want to record — you're free to use what's appropriate for you.

Here are some hints about how to measure and record particular items:

Weight. Your actual weight won't fluctuate appreciably in 24 hours, although scale weight may vary as much as 5-8 pounds depending on your state of hydration. If you are training hard every day or riding a lengthy stage race, daily weight checks will help you determine if you are adequately replacing lost fluids. But during normal training, morning weigh-ins are unnecessay. Instead, step on the scale about once or twice a week to check for trends. A steady decrease past your best racing weight may indicate that you are dipping into muscle reserves and in danger of falling victim to overtraining.

Heart Rate. Take this immediately after waking up and, if you are training seriously, again when you actually get up. The difference between the two rates is an indicator of your fitness. For example if the difference betwen the two rates is suddenly 8 or 10 beats above your norm, it's a sign you may not have recovered from the previous day's effort.

Don't forget the newcomer to fitness will see his resting heart rate fall steadily during the initial months of training, from about 75 beats per minute in sedentary life to the low 50s as exercise strengthens the cardiovascular system and makes it more efficient. Once it reaches a stable rate (determined by heredity as well as training volume) there is usually no need to check it frequently. The exception is during periods of heavy training, especially when you are doing intervals. Then heart rate should be recorded daily because an increase (at rest) of more than five or six beats may be signaling problems. Remember that a variation can be caused by so many factors that it is not a very reliable indicator of overtraining, though it certainly won't hurt to see if daily pulse checks have any predictive value for you. Here again the importance of recording exact figures over several years is obvious.

Workout. Record what you do on the bike each day. Note miles, route, gears, and cadence, along with any special features of the ride, such as intervals, riding companions, and weather conditions. Also include data on any timed sections.

Remarks. This pertains to things not related directly to cycling. Included are happenings in your off-the-bike life that can affect either training or racing performance, such as job or school stress, staying up late at night, illness and injuries, changes in diet, etc. Example: "Tired last 20 miles from bout with flu Monday. Felt okay rest of day."

Make note of any special mechanical circumstances like saddle or handlebar height adjustments, new components or wheels, and clothing. For instance, unfamiliar shoes can cause knee trouble if the cleats vary the position of the foot on the pedal. Even if the resulting irritation is barely noticeable after one ride, the training diary helps you spot the pattern.

Although the information you keep in this training diary will help you plan future workouts, it may also bring you unexpected pleasures in the years to come. It will be a memento of the enjoyable and productive hours you spent improving your health and increasing your strength and skills in the unique and wonderful sport of bicycling.

— Adapted from Fred Matheny's
Beginning Bicycle Racing

SAMPLE ENTRY

Saturday *Sept. 4*
Hrs. Sleeping *7½* Weight *163* Pulse/Waking *50* Rising *62* Diff *12*
Nutrition *B: Granola, milk, banana, tea L: 2 BLT's*
D: spaghetti, salad, bread, ice-cream, a beer Snack: apple
Distance ridden today *70 miles* Workout type *LSD*
Course *Rolling hills for 3/4; flat for 1/4 — two steep*
hills about 1/2 way.
_____ Weather *Cool/ 60's*
Remarks *Rode 42 x 16, 17. 2 Hill jams. Felt good,*
but not real strong. Kept it steady. No knee
problems.

Gear Ratio Chart (for 27 inch wheels)

Number of teeth on rear sprocket

Number of teeth on chain ring

	12	13	14	15	16	17	18	19	20	21	22	23	24	25	26	27	28	
39	87.8	81.0	75.2	70.2	65.8	61.9	58.5	55.4	52.6	50.1	47.9	45.8	43.9	42.1	40.5	39.0	37.6	39
40	90.0	83.0	77.1	72.0	67.5	63.5	60.0	56.8	54.0	51.4	49.1	47.0	45.0	43.2	41.5	40.0	38.6	40
41	92.2	85.1	79.0	73.8	69.1	65.1	61.5	58.2	55.3	52.7	50.3	48.1	46.1	44.2	42.4	41.0	39.5	41
42	94.5	87.2	81.0	75.6	70.8	66.7	63.0	59.6	56.7	54.0	51.5	49.3	47.2	45.3	43.6	42.0	40.5	42
43	96.7	89.3	82.9	77.4	72.5	68.2	64.4	61.1	58.1	55.2	52.8	50.4	48.3	46.4	44.6	43.0	41.4	43
44	99.0	91.3	84.9	79.2	74.3	69.9	66.0	62.5	59.4	56.6	54.0	51.6	49.5	47.5	45.7	44.0	42.4	44
45	101.3	93.4	86.7	81.0	76.0	71.5	67.5	64.0	60.8	57.9	55.2	52.8	50.7	48.6	46.7	45.0	43.4	45
46	103.5	95.5	88.7	82.8	77.6	73.1	69.0	65.4	62.1	59.1	56.5	54.0	51.8	49.7	47.8	46.0	44.4	46
47	105.7	97.6	90.6	84.6	79.3	74.6	70.5	66.8	63.4	60.4	57.6	55.2	52.9	50.8	48.8	47.0	45.3	47
48	108.0	99.6	92.6	86.4	81.0	76.2	72.0	68.2	64.8	61.7	58.9	56.3	54.0	51.8	49.9	48.0	46.3	48
49	110.2	101.7	94.5	88.2	82.7	77.8	73.5	69.6	66.2	63.0	60.1	57.5	55.1	52.9	50.9	49.0	47.2	49
50	112.5	103.8	96.4	90.0	84.4	79.4	75.0	71.0	67.5	64.3	61.4	58.7	56.3	54.0	51.9	50.0	48.2	50
51	114.8	105.3	98.4	91.8	86.1	81.0	76.5	72.5	68.8	65.6	62.6	59.9	57.4	55.1	53.0	51.0	49.2	51
52	117.0	108.0	100.3	93.6	87.8	82.6	78.0	73.9	70.2	66.9	63.8	61.0	58.5	56.2	54.0	52.0	50.1	52
53	119.2	110.0	102.2	95.4	89.4	84.1	79.5	75.3	71.5	68.1	65.0	62.2	59.6	57.2	55.0	53.0	51.1	53
54	121.5	112.2	104.1	97.2	91.1	85.8	81.0	76.7	72.9	69.4	66.3	63.4	60.8	58.3	56.1	54.0	52.1	54
55	123.7	114.2	106.1	99.0	92.8	87.4	82.5	78.2	74.3	70.7	67.5	64.6	61.9	59.4	57.1	55.0	53.0	55
	12	13	14	15	16	17	18	19	20	21	22	23	24	25	26	27	28	

The numbers on this chart are figured by dividing the number of front teeth by the number of rear teeth and multiplying by the number of inches in diameter of the wheel (27 inches for most adult racing bicycles.).

Calculations:

Week of _____

Monday _____
Hrs. Sleeping _____ Weight _____ Pulse/Waking _____ Rising _____ Diff _____
Nutrition _____

_____

Distance ridden today _____ Workout type _____
Course _____

_____
_____ Weather _____
Remarks _____

_____
_____
_____

Tuesday _____
Hrs. Sleeping _____ Weight _____ Pulse/Waking _____ Rising _____ Diff _____
Nutrition _____

_____

Distance ridden today _____ Workout type _____
Course _____

_____
_____ Weather _____
Remarks _____

_____
_____
_____

Wednesday _____
Hrs. Sleeping _____ Weight _____ Pulse/Waking _____ Rising _____ Diff _____
Nutrition _____

_____

Distance ridden today _____ Workout type _____
Course _____

_____
_____ Weather _____
Remarks _____

_____
_____
_____

Thursday _____

Hrs. Sleeping _____ Weight _____ Pulse/Waking _____ Rising _____ Diff _____

Nutrition _____

_____

Distance ridden today _____ Workout type _____

Course _____

_____

_____ Weather _____

Remarks _____

_____

_____

_____

Friday _____

Hrs. Sleeping _____ Weight _____ Pulse/Waking _____ Rising _____ Diff _____

Nutrition _____

_____

Distance ridden today _____ Workout type _____

Course _____

_____

_____ Weather _____

Remarks _____

_____

_____

_____

Saturday _____

Hrs. Sleeping _____ Weight _____ Pulse/Waking _____ Rising _____ Diff _____

Nutrition _____

_____

Distance ridden today _____ Workout type _____

Course _____

_____

_____ Weather _____

Remarks _____

_____

_____

_____

Sunday _____

Hrs. Sleeping _____ Weight _____ Pulse/Waking _____ Rising _____ Diff _____

Nutrition _____

_____

Distance ridden today _____ Workout type _____

Course _____

_____

_____ Weather _____

Remarks _____

_____

_____

_____

Race

Date _____ Time of Start _____ Event _____

Distance _____ Category ridden _____

Placing _____ Time _____

Competition _____

_____

Weather _____

Equipment _____

_____

Remarks _____

_____

_____

Weekly Summary

Distance this week _____

Mechanical notes _____

_____

_____

Remarks _____

_____

_____

_____

_____

Week of _____

Monday _____

Hrs. Sleeping _____ Weight _____ Pulse/Waking _____ Rising _____ Diff _____

Nutrition _____
_____

Distance ridden today _____ Workout type _____

Course _____
_____
_____ Weather _____

Remarks _____
_____
_____
_____

Tuesday _____

Hrs. Sleeping _____ Weight _____ Pulse/Waking _____ Rising _____ Diff _____

Nutrition _____
_____

Distance ridden today _____ Workout type _____

Course _____
_____
_____ Weather _____

Remarks _____
_____
_____
_____

Wednesday _____

Hrs. Sleeping _____ Weight _____ Pulse/Waking _____ Rising _____ Diff _____

Nutrition _____
_____

Distance ridden today _____ Workout type _____

Course _____
_____
_____ Weather _____

Remarks _____
_____
_____
_____

> 'As miserable as I got,
> I never thought of turning back.
> I did think, though, of my old,
> good friend, the small chainring.'

Thursday _____

Hrs. Sleeping _____ Weight _____ Pulse/Waking _____ Rising _____ Diff _____

Nutrition _____

_____

Distance ridden today _____ Workout type _____

Course _____

_____

_____ Weather _____

Remarks _____

_____

_____

_____

Friday _____

Hrs. Sleeping _____ Weight _____ Pulse/Waking _____ Rising _____ Diff _____

Nutrition _____

_____

Distance ridden today _____ Workout type _____

Course _____

_____

_____ Weather _____

Remarks _____

_____

_____

_____

Laura Charameda and Linda Brenneman leading sprint at the 1993 Dole criterium in Visalia, Califonia.

Saturday _____

Hrs. Sleeping _____ Weight _____ Pulse/Waking _____ Rising _____ Diff _____
Nutrition _____
_____

Distance ridden today _____ Workout type _____
Course _____
_____
_____ Weather _____
Remarks _____
_____
_____
_____

Sunday _____

Hrs. Sleeping _____ Weight _____ Pulse/Waking _____ Rising _____ Diff _____

Nutrition _____

_____

Distance ridden today _____ Workout type _____

Course _____

_____

_____ Weather _____

Remarks _____

_____

_____

_____

Race

Date _____ Time of Start _____ Event _____

Distance _____ Category ridden _____

Placing _____ Time _____

Competition _____

_____

Weather _____

Equipment _____

_____

Remarks _____

_____

_____

Weekly Summary

Distance this week _____

Mechanical notes _____

_____

_____

_____

Remarks _____

_____

_____

_____

_____

_____

Week of _____

Monday _____

Hrs. Sleeping _____ Weight _____ Pulse/Waking _____ Rising _____ Diff _____

Nutrition _____

_____

Distance ridden today _____ Workout type _____

Course _____

_____

_____ Weather _____

Remarks _____

_____

_____

_____

Tuesday _____

Hrs. Sleeping _____ Weight _____ Pulse/Waking _____ Rising _____ Diff _____

Nutrition _____

_____

Distance ridden today _____ Workout type _____

Course _____

_____

_____ Weather _____

Remarks _____

_____

_____

_____

Wednesday _____

Hrs. Sleeping _____ Weight _____ Pulse/Waking _____ Rising _____ Diff _____

Nutrition _____

_____

Distance ridden today _____ Workout type _____

Course _____

_____

_____ Weather _____

Remarks _____

_____

_____

_____

Thursday _____

Hrs. Sleeping _____ Weight _____ Pulse/Waking _____ Rising _____ Diff _____

Nutrition _____

_____

Distance ridden today _____ Workout type _____

Course _____

_____

_____ Weather _____

Remarks _____

_____

_____

_____

Friday _____

Hrs. Sleeping _____ Weight _____ Pulse/Waking _____ Rising _____ Diff _____

Nutrition _____

_____

Distance ridden today _____ Workout type _____

Course _____

_____

_____ Weather _____

Remarks _____

_____

_____

_____

Saturday _____

Hrs. Sleeping _____ Weight _____ Pulse/Waking _____ Rising _____ Diff _____

Nutrition _____

_____

Distance ridden today _____ Workout type _____

Course _____

_____

_____ Weather _____

Remarks _____

_____

_____

_____

Sunday _____

Hrs. Sleeping _____ Weight _____ Pulse/Waking _____ Rising _____ Diff _____

Nutrition _____

_____

Distance ridden today _____ Workout type _____

Course _____

_____

_____ Weather _____

Remarks _____

_____

_____

_____

Race

Date _____ Time of Start _____ Event _____

Distance _____ Category ridden _____

Placing _____ Time _____

Competition _____

_____

Weather _____

Equipment _____

_____

Remarks _____

_____

_____

Weekly Summary

Distance this week _____

Mechanical notes _____

_____

_____

_____

Remarks _____

_____

_____

_____

_____

Week of _____

Monday _____
Hrs. Sleeping _____ Weight _____ Pulse/Waking _____ Rising _____ Diff _____
Nutrition _____

_____
Distance ridden today _____ Workout type _____
Course _____

_____
_____ Weather _____
Remarks _____

_____
_____
_____

Tuesday _____
Hrs. Sleeping _____ Weight _____ Pulse/Waking _____ Rising _____ Diff _____
Nutrition _____

_____
Distance ridden today _____ Workout type _____
Course _____

_____
_____ Weather _____
Remarks _____

_____
_____
_____

Wednesday _____
Hrs. Sleeping _____ Weight _____ Pulse/Waking _____ Rising _____ Diff _____
Nutrition _____

_____
Distance ridden today _____ Workout type _____
Course _____

_____
_____ Weather _____
Remarks _____

_____
_____
_____

Thursday _____

Hrs. Sleeping _____ Weight _____ Pulse/Waking _____ Rising _____ Diff _____

Nutrition _____

_____

Distance ridden today _____ Workout type _____

Course _____

_____

_____ Weather _____

Remarks _____

_____

_____

_____

Friday _____

Hrs. Sleeping _____ Weight _____ Pulse/Waking _____ Rising _____ Diff _____

Nutrition _____

_____

Distance ridden today _____ Workout type _____

Course _____

_____

_____ Weather _____

Remarks _____

_____

_____

_____

Saturday _____

Hrs. Sleeping _____ Weight _____ Pulse/Waking _____ Rising _____ Diff _____

Nutrition _____

_____

Distance ridden today _____ Workout type _____

Course _____

_____

_____ Weather _____

Remarks _____

_____

_____

_____

Sunday _____

Hrs. Sleeping _____ Weight _____ Pulse/Waking _____ Rising _____ Diff _____

Nutrition _____

_____

Distance ridden today _____ Workout type _____

Course _____

_____

_____ Weather _____

Remarks _____

_____

_____

_____

Race

Date _____ Time of Start _____ Event _____

Distance _____ Category ridden _____

Placing _____ Time _____

Competition _____

_____

Weather _____

Equipment _____

_____

Remarks _____

_____

_____

Weekly Summary

Distance this week _____

Mechanical notes _____

_____

_____

_____

Remarks _____

_____

_____

_____

_____

_____

Week of _____

Monday _____

Hrs. Sleeping _____ Weight _____ Pulse/Waking _____ Rising _____ Diff _____

Nutrition _____

_____

Distance ridden today _____ Workout type _____

Course _____

_____

_____ Weather _____

Remarks _____

_____

_____

_____

Tuesday _____

Hrs. Sleeping _____ Weight _____ Pulse/Waking _____ Rising _____ Diff _____

Nutrition _____

_____

Distance ridden today _____ Workout type _____

Course _____

_____

_____ Weather _____

Remarks _____

_____

_____

_____

Wednesday _____

Hrs. Sleeping _____ Weight _____ Pulse/Waking _____ Rising _____ Diff _____

Nutrition _____

_____

Distance ridden today _____ Workout type _____

Course _____

_____

_____ Weather _____

Remarks _____

_____

_____

_____

Thursday _____

Hrs. Sleeping _____ Weight _____ Pulse/Waking _____ Rising _____ Diff _____

Nutrition _____

_____

Distance ridden today _____ Workout type _____

Course _____

_____

_____ Weather _____

Remarks _____

_____

_____

_____

Friday _____

Hrs. Sleeping _____ Weight _____ Pulse/Waking _____ Rising _____ Diff _____

Nutrition _____

_____

Distance ridden today _____ Workout type _____

Course _____

_____

_____ Weather _____

Remarks _____

_____

_____

_____

Saturday _____

Hrs. Sleeping _____ Weight _____ Pulse/Waking _____ Rising _____ Diff _____

Nutrition _____

_____

Distance ridden today _____ Workout type _____

Course _____

_____

_____ Weather _____

Remarks _____

_____

_____

_____

Sunday _____

Hrs. Sleeping _____ Weight _____ Pulse/Waking _____ Rising _____ Diff _____

Nutrition _____

_____

Distance ridden today _____ Workout type _____

Course _____

_____

_____ Weather _____

Remarks _____

_____

_____

_____

Race

Date _____ Time of Start _____ Event _____

Distance _____ Category ridden _____

Placing _____ Time _____

Competition _____

_____

Weather _____

Equipment _____

_____

Remarks _____

_____

_____

Weekly Summary

Distance this week _____

Mechanical notes _____

_____

_____

_____

Remarks _____

_____

_____

_____

_____

_____

Week of _____

Monday _____

Hrs. Sleeping _____Weight _____Pulse/Waking _____Rising _____Diff _____

Nutrition _____

_____

Distance ridden today _____Workout type _____

Course _____

_____

_____ Weather _____

Remarks _____

_____

_____

_____

Tuesday _____

Hrs. Sleeping _____Weight _____Pulse/Waking _____Rising _____Diff _____

Nutrition _____

_____

Distance ridden today _____Workout type _____

Course _____

_____

_____ Weather _____

Remarks _____

_____

_____

_____

Wednesday _____

Hrs. Sleeping _____Weight _____Pulse/Waking _____Rising _____Diff _____

Nutrition _____

_____

Distance ridden today _____Workout type _____

Course _____

_____

_____ Weather _____

Remarks _____

_____

_____

_____

Thursday _____
Hrs. Sleeping _____ Weight _____ Pulse/Waking _____ Rising _____ Diff _____
Nutrition _____
_____
Distance ridden today _____ Workout type _____
Course _____
_____
_____ Weather _____
Remarks _____
_____
_____
_____

Friday _____
Hrs. Sleeping _____ Weight _____ Pulse/Waking _____ Rising _____ Diff _____
Nutrition _____
_____
Distance ridden today _____ Workout type _____
Course _____
_____
_____ Weather _____
Remarks _____
_____
_____
_____

Saturday _____
Hrs. Sleeping _____ Weight _____ Pulse/Waking _____ Rising _____ Diff _____
Nutrition _____
_____
Distance ridden today _____ Workout type _____
Course _____
_____
_____ Weather _____
Remarks _____
_____
_____
_____

Sunday _____

Hrs. Sleeping _____ Weight _____ Pulse/Waking _____ Rising _____ Diff _____

Nutrition _____

_____

Distance ridden today _____ Workout type _____

Course _____

_____

_____ Weather _____

Remarks _____

_____

_____

_____

Race

Date _____ Time of Start _____ Event _____

Distance _____ Category ridden _____

Placing _____ Time _____

Competition _____

_____

Weather _____

Equipment _____

_____

Remarks _____

_____

_____

Weekly Summary

Distance this week _____

Mechanical notes _____

_____

_____

_____

Remarks _____

_____

_____

_____

_____

_____

Week of _____

Monday _____

Hrs. Sleeping _____ Weight _____ Pulse/Waking _____ Rising _____ Diff _____

Nutrition _____

_____

Distance ridden today _____ Workout type _____

Course _____

_____

_____ Weather _____

Remarks _____

_____

_____

_____

Tuesday _____

Hrs. Sleeping _____ Weight _____ Pulse/Waking _____ Rising _____ Diff _____

Nutrition _____

_____

Distance ridden today _____ Workout type _____

Course _____

_____

_____ Weather _____

Remarks _____

_____

_____

_____

Wednesday _____

Hrs. Sleeping _____ Weight _____ Pulse/Waking _____ Rising _____ Diff _____

Nutrition _____

_____

Distance ridden today _____ Workout type _____

Course _____

_____

_____ Weather _____

Remarks _____

_____

_____

_____

Thursday _____

Hrs. Sleeping _____ Weight _____ Pulse/Waking _____ Rising _____ Diff _____

Nutrition _____

_____

Distance ridden today _____ Workout type _____

Course _____

_____

_____ Weather _____

Remarks _____

_____

_____

_____

*'Miles without quality
won't cut it anymore.'*

Friday _____

Hrs. Sleeping _____ Weight _____ Pulse/Waking _____ Rising _____ Diff _____

Nutrition _____

_____

Distance ridden today _____ Workout type _____

Course _____

_____

_____ Weather _____

Remarks _____

_____

_____

_____

Saturday ―――――――――――――――

Hrs. Sleeping _____ Weight _____ Pulse/Waking _____ Rising _____ Diff _____

Nutrition _____

_____

Distance ridden today _____ Workout type _____

Course _____

_____ Weather _____

Remarks _____

_____

_____

_____

Coors Light pro Roy Knickman on the cobbles in the 1993 Tour Dupont.

Sunday _____

Hrs. Sleeping _____ Weight _____ Pulse/Waking _____ Rising _____ Diff _____

Nutrition _____

Distance ridden today _____ Workout type _____

Course _____

_____ Weather _____

Remarks _____

_____

_____

_____

Race

Date _____ Time of Start _____ Event _____

Distance _____ Category ridden _____

Placing_____ Time _____

Competition _____

Weather _____

Equipment _____

Remarks _____

_____

_____

Weekly Summary

Distance this week _____

Mechanical notes _____

_____

_____

_____

Remarks _____

_____

_____

_____

_____

_____

Week of _____

Monday _____

Hrs. Sleeping _____ Weight _____ Pulse/Waking _____ Rising _____ Diff _____

Nutrition _____

_____

Distance ridden today _____ Workout type _____

Course _____

_____

_____ Weather _____

Remarks _____

_____

_____

_____

Tuesday _____

Hrs. Sleeping _____ Weight _____ Pulse/Waking _____ Rising _____ Diff _____

Nutrition _____

_____

Distance ridden today _____ Workout type _____

Course _____

_____

_____ Weather _____

Remarks _____

_____

_____

_____

Wednesday _____

Hrs. Sleeping _____ Weight _____ Pulse/Waking _____ Rising _____ Diff _____

Nutrition _____

_____

Distance ridden today _____ Workout type _____

Course _____

_____

_____ Weather _____

Remarks _____

_____

_____

_____

Thursday _____
Hrs. Sleeping _____ Weight _____ Pulse/Waking _____ Rising _____ Diff _____
Nutrition _____
_____

Distance ridden today _____ Workout type _____
Course _____
_____
_____ Weather _____
Remarks _____
_____
_____
_____

Friday _____
Hrs. Sleeping _____ Weight _____ Pulse/Waking _____ Rising _____ Diff _____
Nutrition _____
_____

Distance ridden today _____ Workout type _____
Course _____
_____
_____ Weather _____
Remarks _____
_____
_____
_____

Saturday _____
Hrs. Sleeping _____ Weight _____ Pulse/Waking _____ Rising _____ Diff _____
Nutrition _____
_____

Distance ridden today _____ Workout type _____
Course _____
_____
_____ Weather _____
Remarks _____
_____
_____
_____

Sunday _____

Hrs. Sleeping _____ Weight _____ Pulse/Waking _____ Rising _____ Diff _____

Nutrition _____

_____

Distance ridden today _____ Workout type _____

Course _____

_____

_____ Weather _____

Remarks _____

_____

_____

_____

Race

Date _____ Time of Start _____ Event _____

Distance _____ Category ridden _____

Placing _____ Time _____

Competition _____

_____

Weather _____

Equipment _____

_____

Remarks _____

_____

_____

Weekly Summary

Distance this week _____

Mechanical notes _____

_____

_____

_____

Remarks _____

_____

_____

_____

_____

_____

Week of _____

Monday _____

Hrs. Sleeping _____ Weight _____ Pulse/Waking _____ Rising _____ Diff _____

Nutrition _____

_____

Distance ridden today _____ Workout type _____

Course _____

_____

_____ Weather _____

Remarks _____

_____

_____

_____

Tuesday _____

Hrs. Sleeping _____ Weight _____ Pulse/Waking _____ Rising _____ Diff _____

Nutrition _____

_____

Distance ridden today _____ Workout type _____

Course _____

_____

_____ Weather _____

Remarks _____

_____

_____

_____

Wednesday _____

Hrs. Sleeping _____ Weight _____ Pulse/Waking _____ Rising _____ Diff _____

Nutrition _____

_____

Distance ridden today _____ Workout type _____

Course _____

_____

_____ Weather _____

Remarks _____

_____

_____

_____

Thursday _____

Hrs. Sleeping _____ Weight _____ Pulse/Waking _____ Rising _____ Diff _____

Nutrition _____
_____

Distance ridden today _____ Workout type _____
Course _____
_____
_____ Weather _____
Remarks _____
_____
_____
_____

Friday _____

Hrs. Sleeping _____ Weight _____ Pulse/Waking _____ Rising _____ Diff _____

Nutrition _____
_____

Distance ridden today _____ Workout type _____
Course _____
_____
_____ Weather _____
Remarks _____
_____
_____
_____

Saturday _____

Hrs. Sleeping _____ Weight _____ Pulse/Waking _____ Rising _____ Diff _____

Nutrition _____
_____

Distance ridden today _____ Workout type _____
Course _____
_____
_____ Weather _____
Remarks _____
_____
_____
_____

Sunday _____

Hrs. Sleeping _____ Weight _____ Pulse/Waking _____ Rising _____ Diff _____

Nutrition _____

_____

Distance ridden today _____ Workout type _____

Course _____

_____

_____ Weather _____

Remarks _____

_____

_____

_____

Race

Date _____ Time of Start _____ Event _____

Distance _____ Category ridden _____

Placing _____ Time _____

Competition _____

_____

Weather _____

Equipment _____

_____

Remarks _____

_____

_____

Weekly Summary

Distance this week _____

Mechanical notes _____

_____

_____

_____

Remarks _____

_____

_____

_____

_____

_____

Week of _____

Monday _____
Hrs. Sleeping _____ Weight _____ Pulse/Waking _____ Rising _____ Diff _____
Nutrition _____

_____
Distance ridden today _____ Workout type _____
Course _____

_____
_____ Weather _____
Remarks _____

_____
_____
_____

Tuesday _____
Hrs. Sleeping _____ Weight _____ Pulse/Waking _____ Rising _____ Diff _____
Nutrition _____

_____
Distance ridden today _____ Workout type _____
Course _____

_____
_____ Weather _____
Remarks _____

_____
_____
_____

Wednesday _____
Hrs. Sleeping _____ Weight _____ Pulse/Waking _____ Rising _____ Diff _____
Nutrition _____

_____
Distance ridden today _____ Workout type _____
Course _____

_____
_____ Weather _____
Remarks _____

_____
_____
_____

*'He knew for certain that
Alfredo Binda was, at one time,
more than a name on a toestrap.'*

Thursday _____
Hrs. Sleeping _____ Weight _____ Pulse/Waking _____ Rising _____ Diff _____
Nutrition _____
_____
Distance ridden today _____ Workout type _____
Course _____
_____
_____ Weather _____
Remarks _____
_____
_____
_____

Friday _____
Hrs. Sleeping _____ Weight _____ Pulse/Waking _____ Rising _____ Diff _____
Nutrition _____
_____
Distance ridden today _____ Workout type _____
Course _____
_____
_____ Weather _____
Remarks _____
_____
_____
_____

Saturday _____

Hrs. Sleeping _____ Weight _____ Pulse/Waking _____ Rising _____ Diff _____

Nutrition _____

_____

Distance ridden today _____ Workout type _____

Course _____

_____

_____ Weather _____

Remarks _____

_____

_____

_____

Echelons in the 1990 Ruta Mexico.

Sunday _____

Hrs. Sleeping _____ Weight _____ Pulse/Waking _____ Rising _____ Diff _____

Nutrition _____

_____

Distance ridden today _____ Workout type _____

Course _____

_____

_____ Weather _____

Remarks _____

_____

_____

_____

Race

Date _____ Time of Start _____ Event _____

Distance _____ Category ridden _____

Placing_____ Time _____

Competition _____

_____

Weather _____

Equipment_____

_____

Remarks _____

_____

_____

Weekly Summary

Distance this week _____

Mechanical notes _____

_____

_____

_____

Remarks_____

_____

_____

_____

_____

_____

Week of _____

Monday _____
Hrs. Sleeping _____Weight _____Pulse/Waking _____Rising _____Diff _____
Nutrition _____
_____

Distance ridden today _____Workout type _____
Course _____
_____
_____ Weather _____
Remarks _____
_____
_____
_____

Tuesday _____
Hrs. Sleeping _____Weight _____Pulse/Waking _____Rising _____Diff _____
Nutrition _____
_____

Distance ridden today _____Workout type _____
Course _____
_____
_____ Weather _____
Remarks _____
_____
_____
_____

Wednesday _____
Hrs. Sleeping _____Weight _____Pulse/Waking _____Rising _____Diff _____
Nutrition _____
_____

Distance ridden today _____Workout type _____
Course _____
_____
_____ Weather _____
Remarks _____
_____
_____
_____

Thursday _____

Hrs. Sleeping _____ Weight _____ Pulse/Waking _____ Rising _____ Diff _____

Nutrition _____

_____

Distance ridden today _____ Workout type _____

Course _____

_____

_____ Weather _____

Remarks _____

_____

_____

_____

Friday _____

Hrs. Sleeping _____ Weight _____ Pulse/Waking _____ Rising _____ Diff _____

Nutrition _____

_____

Distance ridden today _____ Workout type _____

Course _____

_____

_____ Weather _____

Remarks _____

_____

_____

_____

Saturday _____

Hrs. Sleeping _____ Weight _____ Pulse/Waking _____ Rising _____ Diff _____

Nutrition _____

_____

Distance ridden today _____ Workout type _____

Course _____

_____

_____ Weather _____

Remarks _____

_____

_____

_____

Sunday _____

Hrs. Sleeping _____ Weight _____ Pulse/Waking _____ Rising _____ Diff _____

Nutrition _____

_____

Distance ridden today _____ Workout type _____

Course _____

_____

_____ Weather _____

Remarks _____

_____

_____

_____

Race

Date _____ Time of Start _____ Event _____

Distance _____ Category ridden _____

Placing_____ Time _____

Competition _____

_____

Weather _____

Equipment_____

_____

Remarks _____

_____

_____

Weekly Summary

Distance this week _____

Mechanical notes _____

_____

_____

_____

Remarks_____

_____

_____

_____

_____

_____

Week of _____

Monday _____

Hrs. Sleeping _____ Weight _____ Pulse/Waking _____ Rising _____ Diff _____

Nutrition _____

_____

Distance ridden today _____ Workout type _____

Course _____

_____

_____ Weather _____

Remarks _____

_____

_____

_____

Tuesday _____

Hrs. Sleeping _____ Weight _____ Pulse/Waking _____ Rising _____ Diff _____

Nutrition _____

_____

Distance ridden today _____ Workout type _____

Course _____

_____

_____ Weather _____

Remarks _____

_____

_____

_____

Wednesday _____

Hrs. Sleeping _____ Weight _____ Pulse/Waking _____ Rising _____ Diff _____

Nutrition _____

_____

Distance ridden today _____ Workout type _____

Course _____

_____

_____ Weather _____

Remarks _____

_____

_____

_____

Thursday _____

Hrs. Sleeping _____ Weight _____ Pulse/Waking _____ Rising _____ Diff _____

Nutrition _____

_____

Distance ridden today _____ Workout type _____

Course _____

_____

_____ Weather _____

Remarks _____

_____

_____

_____

Friday _____

Hrs. Sleeping _____ Weight _____ Pulse/Waking _____ Rising _____ Diff _____

Nutrition _____

_____

Distance ridden today _____ Workout type _____

Course _____

_____

_____ Weather _____

Remarks _____

_____

_____

Saturday _____

Hrs. Sleeping _____ Weight _____ Pulse/Waking _____ Rising _____ Diff _____

Nutrition _____

_____

Distance ridden today _____ Workout type _____

Course _____

_____

_____ Weather _____

Remarks _____

_____

_____

_____

Sunday _____

Hrs. Sleeping _____ Weight _____ Pulse/Waking _____ Rising _____ Diff _____

Nutrition _____

_____

Distance ridden today _____ Workout type _____

Course _____

_____

_____ Weather _____

Remarks _____

_____

_____

_____

Race

Date _____ Time of Start _____ Event _____

Distance _____ Category ridden _____

Placing _____ Time _____

Competition _____

_____

Weather _____

Equipment _____

_____

Remarks _____

_____

_____

Weekly Summary

Distance this week _____

Mechanical notes _____

_____

_____

_____

Remarks _____

_____

_____

_____

_____

_____

Week of _____

Monday _____
Hrs. Sleeping _____Weight _____Pulse/Waking _____Rising _____Diff _____
Nutrition _____
_____
Distance ridden today _____Workout type _____
Course _____
_____
_____ Weather _____
Remarks _____
_____
_____
_____

Tuesday _____
Hrs. Sleeping _____Weight _____Pulse/Waking _____Rising _____Diff _____
Nutrition _____
_____
Distance ridden today _____Workout type _____
Course _____
_____
_____ Weather _____
Remarks _____
_____
_____
_____

Wednesday _____
Hrs. Sleeping _____Weight _____Pulse/Waking _____Rising _____Diff _____
Nutrition _____
_____
Distance ridden today _____Workout type _____
Course _____
_____
_____ Weather _____
Remarks _____
_____
_____
_____

Thursday _____

Hrs. Sleeping _____ Weight _____ Pulse/Waking _____ Rising _____ Diff _____

Nutrition _____

_____

Distance ridden today _____ Workout type _____

Course _____

_____

_____ Weather _____

Remarks _____

_____

_____

_____

Friday _____

Hrs. Sleeping _____ Weight _____ Pulse/Waking _____ Rising _____ Diff _____

Nutrition _____

_____

Distance ridden today _____ Workout type _____

Course _____

_____

_____ Weather _____

Remarks _____

_____

_____

_____

Saturday _____

Hrs. Sleeping _____ Weight _____ Pulse/Waking _____ Rising _____ Diff _____

Nutrition _____

_____

Distance ridden today _____ Workout type _____

Course _____

_____

_____ Weather _____

Remarks _____

_____

_____

_____

Sunday _____

Hrs. Sleeping _____ Weight _____ Pulse/Waking _____ Rising _____ Diff _____

Nutrition _____
_____

Distance ridden today _____ Workout type _____

Course _____
_____

_____ Weather _____

Remarks _____
_____
_____
_____

Race

Date _____ Time of Start _____ Event _____

Distance _____ Category ridden _____

Placing _____ Time _____

Competition _____
_____

Weather _____

Equipment _____
_____

Remarks _____
_____
_____

Weekly Summary

Distance this week _____

Mechanical notes _____

_____
_____
_____

Remarks _____
_____
_____
_____
_____
_____

Week of _____

Monday _____
Hrs. Sleeping _____ Weight _____ Pulse/Waking _____ Rising _____ Diff _____
Nutrition _____

Distance ridden today _____ Workout type _____
Course _____

_____ Weather _____
Remarks _____
_____
_____
_____

Tuesday _____
Hrs. Sleeping _____ Weight _____ Pulse/Waking _____ Rising _____ Diff _____
Nutrition _____

Distance ridden today _____ Workout type _____
Course _____

_____ Weather _____
Remarks _____
_____
_____
_____

Wednesday _____
Hrs. Sleeping _____ Weight _____ Pulse/Waking _____ Rising _____ Diff _____
Nutrition _____

Distance ridden today _____ Workout type _____
Course _____

_____ Weather _____
Remarks _____
_____
_____
_____

Thursday _____

Hrs. Sleeping _____ Weight _____ Pulse/Waking _____ Rising _____ Diff _____

Nutrition _____

_____

Distance ridden today _____ Workout type _____.

Course _____

_____

_____ Weather _____

Remarks _____

_____

_____

_____

Friday _____

Hrs. Sleeping _____ Weight _____ Pulse/Waking _____ Rising _____ Diff _____

Nutrition _____

_____

Distance ridden today _____ Workout type _____

Course _____

_____

_____ Weather _____

Remarks _____

_____

_____

Saturday _____

Hrs. Sleeping _____ Weight _____ Pulse/Waking _____ Rising _____ Diff _____

Nutrition _____

_____

Distance ridden today _____ Workout type _____

Course _____

_____

_____ Weather _____

Remarks _____

_____

_____

Sunday _____

Hrs. Sleeping _____ Weight _____ Pulse/Waking _____ Rising _____ Diff _____

Nutrition _____

_____

Distance ridden today _____ Workout type _____

Course _____

_____

_____ Weather _____

Remarks _____

_____

_____

_____

Race

Date _____ Time of Start _____ Event _____

Distance _____ Category ridden _____

Placing _____ Time _____

Competition _____

_____

Weather _____

Equipment _____

_____

Remarks _____

_____

_____

Weekly Summary

Distance this week _____

Mechanical notes _____

_____

_____

_____

Remarks _____

_____

_____

_____

_____

Week of _____

Monday _____

Hrs. Sleeping _____ Weight _____ Pulse/Waking _____ Rising _____ Diff _____

Nutrition _____

_____

Distance ridden today _____ Workout type _____

Course _____

_____

_____ Weather _____

Remarks _____

_____

_____

_____

Tuesday _____

Hrs. Sleeping _____ Weight _____ Pulse/Waking _____ Rising _____ Diff _____

Nutrition _____

_____

Distance ridden today _____ Workout type _____

Course _____

_____

_____ Weather _____

Remarks _____

_____

_____

_____

Wednesday _____

Hrs. Sleeping _____ Weight _____ Pulse/Waking _____ Rising _____ Diff _____

Nutrition _____

_____

Distance ridden today _____ Workout type _____

Course _____

_____

_____ Weather _____

Remarks _____

_____

_____

_____

Thursday _____

Hrs. Sleeping _____ Weight _____ Pulse/Waking _____ Rising _____ Diff _____

Nutrition _____

_____

Distance ridden today _____ Workout type _____

Course _____

_____

_____ Weather _____

Remarks _____

_____

_____

_____

---

*'The effort of trying to hang on
just one landmark farther
made her fast.'*

Friday _____

Hrs. Sleeping _____ Weight _____ Pulse/Waking _____ Rising _____ Diff _____

Nutrition _____

_____

Distance ridden today _____ Workout type _____

Course _____

_____

_____ Weather _____

Remarks _____

_____

_____

_____

Saturday _____

Hrs. Sleeping _____ Weight _____ Pulse/Waking _____ Rising _____ Diff _____

Nutrition _____

_____

Distance ridden today _____ Workout type _____

Course _____

_____

_____ Weather _____

Remarks _____

_____

_____

_____

The field downtown in the 1993 Vuelta de Bisbee, Arizona.

Sunday _____

Hrs. Sleeping _____ Weight _____ Pulse/Waking _____ Rising _____ Diff _____

Nutrition _____

_____

Distance ridden today _____ Workout type _____

Course _____

_____

_____ Weather _____

Remarks _____

_____

_____

_____

Race

Date _____ Time of Start _____ Event _____

Distance _____ Category ridden _____

Placing _____ Time _____

Competition _____

_____

Weather _____

Equipment _____

_____

Remarks _____

_____

_____

Weekly Summary

Distance this week _____

Mechanical notes _____

_____

_____

_____

Remarks _____

_____

_____

_____

_____

_____

Week of _____

Monday _____

Hrs. Sleeping _____Weight _____Pulse/Waking _____Rising _____Diff _____

Nutrition _____

_____

Distance ridden today _____Workout type _____

Course _____

_____

_____Weather _____

Remarks _____

_____

_____

_____

Tuesday _____

Hrs. Sleeping _____Weight _____Pulse/Waking _____Rising _____Diff _____

Nutrition _____

_____

Distance ridden today _____Workout type _____

Course _____

_____

_____Weather _____

Remarks _____

_____

_____

_____

Wednesday _____

Hrs. Sleeping _____Weight _____Pulse/Waking _____Rising _____Diff _____

Nutrition _____

_____

Distance ridden today _____Workout type _____

Course _____

_____

_____Weather _____

Remarks _____

_____

_____

_____

Thursday _____

Hrs. Sleeping _____ Weight _____ Pulse/Waking _____ Rising _____ Diff _____

Nutrition _____

_____

Distance ridden today _____ Workout type _____

Course _____

_____

_____ Weather _____

Remarks _____

_____

_____

_____

Friday _____

Hrs. Sleeping _____ Weight _____ Pulse/Waking _____ Rising _____ Diff _____

Nutrition _____

_____

Distance ridden today _____ Workout type _____

Course _____

_____

_____ Weather _____

Remarks _____

_____

_____

_____

Saturday _____

Hrs. Sleeping _____ Weight _____ Pulse/Waking _____ Rising _____ Diff _____

Nutrition _____

_____

Distance ridden today _____ Workout type _____

Course _____

_____

_____ Weather _____

Remarks _____

_____

_____

_____

Sunday _____

Hrs. Sleeping _____ Weight _____ Pulse/Waking _____ Rising _____ Diff _____

Nutrition _____

_____

Distance ridden today _____ Workout type _____

Course _____

_____

_____ Weather _____

Remarks _____

_____

_____

_____

Race

Date _____ Time of Start _____ Event _____

Distance _____ Category ridden _____

Placing _____ Time _____

Competition _____

_____

Weather _____

Equipment _____

_____

Remarks _____

_____

_____

Weekly Summary

Distance this week _____

Mechanical notes _____

_____

_____

_____

Remarks _____

_____

_____

_____

_____

_____

Week of _____

Monday _____
Hrs. Sleeping _____ Weight _____ Pulse/Waking _____ Rising _____ Diff _____
Nutrition _____

Distance ridden today _____ Workout type _____
Course _____

_____ Weather _____
Remarks _____
_____
_____
_____

Tuesday _____
Hrs. Sleeping _____ Weight _____ Pulse/Waking _____ Rising _____ Diff _____
Nutrition _____

Distance ridden today _____ Workout type _____
Course _____

_____ Weather _____
Remarks _____
_____
_____
_____

Wednesday _____
Hrs. Sleeping _____ Weight _____ Pulse/Waking _____ Rising _____ Diff _____
Nutrition _____

Distance ridden today _____ Workout type _____
Course _____

_____ Weather _____
Remarks _____
_____
_____
_____

Thursday _____

Hrs. Sleeping _____ Weight _____ Pulse/Waking _____ Rising _____ Diff _____

Nutrition _____

_____

Distance ridden today _____ Workout type _____

Course _____

_____

_____ Weather _____

Remarks _____

_____

_____

_____

Friday _____

Hrs. Sleeping _____ Weight _____ Pulse/Waking _____ Rising _____ Diff _____

Nutrition _____

_____

Distance ridden today _____ Workout type _____

Course _____

_____

_____ Weather _____

Remarks _____

_____

_____

_____

Saturday _____

Hrs. Sleeping _____ Weight _____ Pulse/Waking _____ Rising _____ Diff _____

Nutrition _____

_____

Distance ridden today _____ Workout type _____

Course _____

_____

_____ Weather _____

Remarks _____

_____

_____

_____

Sunday _____

Hrs. Sleeping _____ Weight _____ Pulse/Waking _____ Rising _____ Diff _____

Nutrition _____
_____

Distance ridden today _____ Workout type _____

Course _____
_____
_____ Weather _____

Remarks _____
_____
_____
_____

Race

Date _____ Time of Start _____ Event _____

Distance _____ Category ridden _____

Placing _____ Time _____

Competition _____
_____

Weather _____

Equipment _____
_____

Remarks _____
_____
_____

Weekly Summary

Distance this week _____

Mechanical notes _____
_____
_____

Remarks _____
_____
_____
_____
_____
_____

Week of _____

Monday _____
Hrs. Sleeping _____ Weight _____ Pulse/Waking _____ Rising _____ Diff _____
Nutrition _____
_____
Distance ridden today _____ Workout type _____
Course _____
_____
_____ Weather _____
Remarks _____
_____
_____
_____

Tuesday _____
Hrs. Sleeping _____ Weight _____ Pulse/Waking _____ Rising _____ Diff _____
Nutrition _____
_____
Distance ridden today _____ Workout type _____
Course _____
_____
_____ Weather _____
Remarks _____
_____
_____
_____

Wednesday _____
Hrs. Sleeping _____ Weight _____ Pulse/Waking _____ Rising _____ Diff _____
Nutrition _____
_____
Distance ridden today _____ Workout type _____
Course _____
_____
_____ Weather _____
Remarks _____
_____
_____
_____

*'Clearly, a training ride
can be a complicated place to be.
A race is somewhat more elemental.'*

Thursday _____
Hrs. Sleeping _____ Weight _____ Pulse/Waking _____ Rising _____ Diff _____
Nutrition _____
_____
Distance ridden today _____ Workout type _____
Course _____
_____
_____ Weather _____
Remarks _____
_____
_____
_____

Friday _____
Hrs. Sleeping _____ Weight _____ Pulse/Waking _____ Rising _____ Diff _____
Nutrition _____
_____
Distance ridden today _____ Workout type _____
Course _____
_____
_____ Weather _____
Remarks _____
_____
_____
_____

Saturday _____

Hrs. Sleeping _____ Weight _____ Pulse/Waking _____ Rising _____ Diff _____

Nutrition _____

_____

Distance ridden today _____ Workout type _____

Course _____

_____

_____ Weather _____

Remarks _____

_____

_____

_____

Scott Skellenger in the 1992 Olympic track trials in Blaine, Minnesota.

Sunday _____

Hrs. Sleeping _____ Weight _____ Pulse/Waking _____ Rising _____ Diff _____

Nutrition _____

_____

Distance ridden today _____ Workout type _____

Course _____

_____

_____ Weather _____

Remarks _____

_____

_____

_____

Race

Date _____ Time of Start _____ Event _____

Distance _____ Category ridden _____

Placing _____ Time _____

Competition _____

_____

Weather _____

Equipment _____

_____

Remarks _____

_____

_____

Weekly Summary

Distance this week _____

Mechanical notes _____

_____

_____

_____

Remarks _____

_____

_____

_____

_____

_____

Week of _____

Monday _____

Hrs. Sleeping _____ Weight _____ Pulse/Waking _____ Rising _____ Diff _____
Nutrition _____
_____

Distance ridden today _____ Workout type _____
Course _____
_____
_____ Weather _____
Remarks _____
_____
_____
_____

Tuesday _____

Hrs. Sleeping _____ Weight _____ Pulse/Waking _____ Rising _____ Diff _____
Nutrition _____
_____

Distance ridden today _____ Workout type _____
Course _____
_____
_____ Weather _____
Remarks _____
_____
_____
_____

Wednesday _____

Hrs. Sleeping _____ Weight _____ Pulse/Waking _____ Rising _____ Diff _____
Nutrition _____
_____

Distance ridden today _____ Workout type _____
Course _____
_____
_____ Weather _____
Remarks _____
_____
_____
_____

Thursday _____
Hrs. Sleeping _____ Weight _____ Pulse/Waking _____ Rising _____ Diff _____
Nutrition _____
_____

Distance ridden today _____ Workout type _____
Course _____
_____
_____ Weather _____
Remarks _____
_____
_____
_____

Friday _____
Hrs. Sleeping _____ Weight _____ Pulse/Waking _____ Rising _____ Diff _____
Nutrition _____
_____

Distance ridden today _____ Workout type _____
Course _____
_____
_____ Weather _____
Remarks _____
_____
_____

Saturday _____
Hrs. Sleeping _____ Weight _____ Pulse/Waking _____ Rising _____ Diff _____
Nutrition _____
_____

Distance ridden today _____ Workout type _____
Course _____
_____
_____ Weather _____
Remarks _____
_____
_____

Sunday _____

Hrs. Sleeping _____ Weight _____ Pulse/Waking _____ Rising _____ Diff _____

Nutrition _____

_____

Distance ridden today _____ Workout type _____

Course _____

_____

_____ Weather _____

Remarks _____

_____

_____

_____

Race

Date _____ Time of Start _____ Event _____

Distance _____ Category ridden _____

Placing _____ Time _____

Competition _____

_____

Weather _____

Equipment _____

Remarks _____

_____

_____

Weekly Summary

Distance this week _____

Mechanical notes _____

_____

_____

_____

Remarks _____

_____

_____

_____

_____

_____

Week of _____

Monday _____
Hrs. Sleeping _____ Weight _____ Pulse/Waking _____ Rising _____ Diff _____
Nutrition _____
_____

Distance ridden today _____ Workout type _____
Course _____
_____
_____ Weather _____
Remarks _____
_____
_____
_____

Tuesday _____
Hrs. Sleeping _____ Weight _____ Pulse/Waking _____ Rising _____ Diff _____
Nutrition _____
_____

Distance ridden today _____ Workout type _____
Course _____
_____
_____ Weather _____
Remarks _____
_____
_____
_____

Wednesday _____
Hrs. Sleeping _____ Weight _____ Pulse/Waking _____ Rising _____ Diff _____
Nutrition _____
_____

Distance ridden today _____ Workout type _____
Course _____
_____
_____ Weather _____
Remarks _____
_____
_____
_____

Thursday _____

Hrs. Sleeping _____ Weight _____ Pulse/Waking _____ Rising _____ Diff _____

Nutrition _____

_____

Distance ridden today _____ Workout type _____

Course _____

_____

_____ Weather _____

Remarks _____

_____

_____

_____

Friday _____

Hrs. Sleeping _____ Weight _____ Pulse/Waking _____ Rising _____ Diff _____

Nutrition _____

_____

Distance ridden today _____ Workout type _____

Course _____

_____

_____ Weather _____

Remarks _____

_____

_____

_____

Saturday _____

Hrs. Sleeping _____ Weight _____ Pulse/Waking _____ Rising _____ Diff _____

Nutrition _____

_____

Distance ridden today _____ Workout type _____

Course _____

_____

_____ Weather _____

Remarks _____

_____

_____

_____

Sunday _____

Hrs. Sleeping _____ Weight _____ Pulse/Waking _____ Rising _____ Diff _____

Nutrition _____

_____

Distance ridden today _____ Workout type _____

Course _____

_____

_____ Weather _____

Remarks _____

_____

_____

_____

Race

Date _____ Time of Start _____ Event _____

Distance _____ Category ridden _____

Placing _____ Time _____

Competition _____

_____

Weather _____

Equipment _____

_____

Remarks _____

_____

_____

Weekly Summary

Distance this week _____

Mechanical notes _____

_____

_____

_____

Remarks _____

_____

_____

_____

_____

Week of _____

Monday _____
Hrs. Sleeping _____ Weight _____ Pulse/Waking _____ Rising _____ Diff _____
Nutrition _____

_____
Distance ridden today _____ Workout type _____
Course _____

_____
_____ Weather _____
Remarks _____

_____
_____
_____

Tuesday _____
Hrs. Sleeping _____ Weight _____ Pulse/Waking _____ Rising _____ Diff _____
Nutrition _____

_____
Distance ridden today _____ Workout type _____
Course _____

_____
_____ Weather _____
Remarks _____

_____
_____
_____

Wednesday _____
Hrs. Sleeping _____ Weight _____ Pulse/Waking _____ Rising _____ Diff _____
Nutrition _____

_____
Distance ridden today _____ Workout type _____
Course _____

_____
_____ Weather _____
Remarks _____

_____
_____
_____

Thursday _____

Hrs. Sleeping _____ Weight _____ Pulse/Waking _____ Rising _____ Diff _____

Nutrition _____

_____

Distance ridden today _____ Workout type _____

Course _____

_____

_____ Weather _____

Remarks _____

_____

_____

_____

Friday _____

Hrs. Sleeping _____ Weight _____ Pulse/Waking _____ Rising _____ Diff _____

Nutrition _____

_____

Distance ridden today _____ Workout type _____

Course _____

_____

_____ Weather _____

Remarks _____

_____

_____

Saturday _____

Hrs. Sleeping _____ Weight _____ Pulse/Waking _____ Rising _____ Diff _____

Nutrition _____

_____

Distance ridden today _____ Workout type _____

Course _____

_____

_____ Weather _____

Remarks _____

_____

_____

Sunday _____

Hrs. Sleeping _____ Weight _____ Pulse/Waking ___ ____ Rising _____ Diff _____

Nutrition _____

_____

Distance ridden today _____ Workout type _____

Course _____

_____

_____ Weather _____

Remarks _____

_____

_____

_____

Race

Date _____ Time of Start _____ Event _____

Distance _____ Category ridden _____

Placing_____ Time _____

Competition _____

_____

Weather_____

Equipment_____

_____

Remarks_____

_____

_____

Weekly Summary

Distance this week _____

Mechanical notes _____

_____

_____

_____

Remarks_____

_____

_____

_____

_____

Week of _____

Monday _____

Hrs. Sleeping _____ Weight _____ Pulse/Waking _____ Rising _____ Diff _____

Nutrition _____

_____

Distance ridden today _____ Workout type _____

Course _____

_____

_____ Weather _____

Remarks _____

_____

_____

_____

Tuesday _____

Hrs. Sleeping _____ Weight _____ Pulse/Waking _____ Rising _____ Diff _____

Nutrition _____

_____

Distance ridden today _____ Workout type _____

Course _____

_____

_____ Weather _____

Remarks _____

_____

_____

_____

Wednesday _____

Hrs. Sleeping _____ Weight _____ Pulse/Waking _____ Rising _____ Diff _____

Nutrition _____

_____

Distance ridden today _____ Workout type _____

Course _____

_____

_____ Weather _____

Remarks _____

_____

_____

_____

Thursday _____

Hrs. Sleeping _____ Weight _____ Pulse/Waking _____ Rising _____ Diff _____

Nutrition _____

_____

Distance ridden today _____ Workout type _____

Course _____

_____

_____ Weather _____

Remarks _____

_____

_____

_____

Friday _____

Hrs. Sleeping _____ Weight _____ Pulse/Waking _____ Rising _____ Diff _____

Nutrition _____

_____

Distance ridden today _____ Workout type _____

Course _____

_____

_____ Weather _____

Remarks _____

_____

_____

_____

Saturday _____

Hrs. Sleeping _____ Weight _____ Pulse/Waking _____ Rising _____ Diff _____

Nutrition _____

_____

Distance ridden today _____ Workout type _____

Course _____

_____

_____ Weather _____

Remarks _____

_____

_____

_____

Sunday _____

Hrs. Sleeping _____ Weight _____ Pulse/Waking _____ Rising _____ Diff _____

Nutrition _____

_____

Distance ridden today _____ Workout type _____

Course _____

_____

_____ Weather _____

Remarks _____

_____

_____

_____

Race

Date _____ Time of Start _____ Event _____

Distance _____ Category ridden _____

Placing _____ Time _____

Competition _____

_____

Weather _____

Equipment _____

_____

Remarks _____

_____

_____

Weekly Summary

Distance this week _____

Mechanical notes _____

_____

_____

_____

Remarks _____

_____

_____

_____

_____

_____

Week of _____

Monday _____
Hrs. Sleeping _____ Weight _____ Pulse/Waking _____ Rising _____ Diff _____
Nutrition _____
_____
Distance ridden today _____ Workout type _____
Course _____
_____
_____ Weather _____
Remarks _____
_____
_____
_____

Tuesday _____
Hrs. Sleeping _____ Weight _____ Pulse/Waking _____ Rising _____ Diff _____
Nutrition _____
_____
Distance ridden today _____ Workout type _____
Course _____
_____
_____ Weather _____
Remarks _____
_____
_____
_____

Wednesday _____
Hrs. Sleeping _____ Weight _____ Pulse/Waking _____ Rising _____ Diff _____
Nutrition _____
_____
Distance ridden today _____ Workout type _____
Course _____
_____
_____ Weather _____
Remarks _____
_____
_____
_____

Thursday _____

Hrs. Sleeping _____ Weight _____ Pulse/Waking _____ Rising _____ Diff _____

Nutrition _____
_____

Distance ridden today _____ Workout type _____

Course _____
_____

_____ Weather _____

Remarks _____
_____
_____
_____

Friday _____

Hrs. Sleeping _____ Weight _____ Pulse/Waking _____ Rising _____ Diff _____

Nutrition _____
_____

Distance ridden today _____ Workout type _____

Course _____
_____

_____ Weather _____

Remarks _____
_____
_____
_____

*'The casual observer gets impressed
by the solo hero effort.
The true aficionado prizes the
unselfish labor of the team player.'*

A road stage in the 1993 Tour Dupont.

Saturday _____

Hrs. Sleeping _____ Weight _____ Pulse/Waking _____ Rising _____ Diff _____
Nutrition _____

Distance ridden today _____ Workout type _____
Course _____

_____ Weather _____
Remarks _____
_____
_____
_____

Sunday _____

Hrs. Sleeping _____ Weight _____ Pulse/Waking _____ Rising _____ Diff _____

Nutrition _____

_____

Distance ridden today _____ Workout type _____

Course _____

_____

_____ Weather _____

Remarks _____

_____

_____

_____

Race

Date _____ Time of Start _____ Event _____

Distance _____ Category ridden _____

Placing _____ Time _____

Competition _____

_____

Weather _____

Equipment _____

_____

Remarks _____

_____

_____

Weekly Summary

Distance this week _____

Mechanical notes _____

_____

_____

_____

Remarks _____

_____

_____

_____

_____

Week of _____

Monday _____
Hrs. Sleeping _____ Weight _____ Pulse/Waking _____ Rising _____ Diff _____
Nutrition _____
_____

Distance ridden today _____ Workout type _____
Course _____
_____
_____ Weather _____
Remarks _____
_____
_____
_____

Tuesday _____
Hrs. Sleeping _____ Weight _____ Pulse/Waking _____ Rising _____ Diff _____
Nutrition _____
_____

Distance ridden today _____ Workout type _____
Course _____
_____
_____ Weather _____
Remarks _____
_____
_____
_____

Wednesday _____
Hrs. Sleeping _____ Weight _____ Pulse/Waking _____ Rising _____ Diff _____
Nutrition _____
_____

Distance ridden today _____ Workout type _____
Course _____
_____
_____ Weather _____
Remarks _____
_____
_____
_____

Thursday _____

Hrs. Sleeping _____ Weight _____ Pulse/Waking _____ Rising _____ Diff _____

Nutrition _____

_____

Distance ridden today _____ Workout type _____

Course _____

_____

_____ Weather _____

Remarks _____

_____

_____

_____

Friday _____

Hrs. Sleeping _____ Weight _____ Pulse/Waking _____ Rising _____ Diff _____

Nutrition _____

_____

Distance ridden today _____ Workout type _____

Course _____

_____

_____ Weather _____

Remarks _____

_____

_____

Saturday _____

Hrs. Sleeping _____ Weight _____ Pulse/Waking _____ Rising _____ Diff _____

Nutrition _____

_____

Distance ridden today _____ Workout type _____

Course _____

_____

_____ Weather _____

Remarks _____

_____

_____

_____

Sunday _____

Hrs. Sleeping _____ Weight _____ Pulse/Waking _____ Rising _____ Diff _____

Nutrition _____

_____

Distance ridden today _____ Workout type _____

Course _____

_____

_____ Weather _____

Remarks _____

_____

_____

_____

Race

Date _____ Time of Start _____ Event _____

Distance _____ Category ridden _____

Placing _____ Time _____

Competition _____

_____

Weather _____

Equipment _____

_____

Remarks _____

_____

_____

Weekly Summary

Distance this week _____

Mechanical notes _____

_____

_____

_____

Remarks _____

_____

_____

_____

_____

Week of _____

Monday _____

Hrs. Sleeping _____ Weight _____ Pulse/Waking _____ Rising _____ Diff _____

Nutrition _____

_____

Distance ridden today _____ Workout type _____

Course _____

_____

_____ Weather _____

Remarks _____

_____

_____

_____

Tuesday _____

Hrs. Sleeping _____ Weight _____ Pulse/Waking _____ Rising _____ Diff _____

Nutrition _____

_____

Distance ridden today _____ Workout type _____

Course _____

_____

_____ Weather _____

Remarks _____

_____

_____

_____

Wednesday _____

Hrs. Sleeping _____ Weight _____ Pulse/Waking _____ Rising _____ Diff _____

Nutrition _____

_____

Distance ridden today _____ Workout type _____

Course _____

_____

_____ Weather _____

Remarks _____

_____

_____

_____

Thursday _____

Hrs. Sleeping _____ Weight _____ Pulse/Waking _____ Rising _____ Diff _____

Nutrition _____

_____

Distance ridden today _____ Workout type _____

Course _____

_____

_____ Weather _____

Remarks _____

_____

_____

_____

Friday _____

Hrs. Sleeping _____ Weight _____ Pulse/Waking _____ Rising _____ Diff _____

Nutrition _____

_____

Distance ridden today _____ Workout type _____

Course _____

_____

_____ Weather _____

Remarks _____

_____

_____

_____

Saturday _____

Hrs. Sleeping _____ Weight _____ Pulse/Waking _____ Rising _____ Diff _____

Nutrition _____

_____

Distance ridden today _____ Workout type _____

Course _____

_____

_____ Weather _____

Remarks _____

_____

_____

_____

Sunday _____

Hrs. Sleeping _____ Weight _____ Pulse/Waking _____ Rising _____ Diff _____

Nutrition _____

_____

Distance ridden today _____ Workout type _____

Course _____

_____

_____ Weather _____

Remarks _____

_____

_____

_____

Race

Date _____ Time of Start _____ Event _____

Distance _____ Category ridden _____

Placing _____ Time _____

Competition _____

_____

Weather _____

Equipment _____

_____

Remarks _____

_____

_____

Weekly Summary

Distance this week _____

Mechanical notes _____

_____

_____

_____

Remarks _____

_____

_____

_____

_____

Week of _____

Monday _____

Hrs. Sleeping _____ Weight _____ Pulse/Waking _____ Rising _____ Diff _____

Nutrition _____

_____

Distance ridden today _____ Workout type _____

Course _____

_____

_____ Weather _____

Remarks _____

_____

_____

_____

Tuesday

Hrs. Sleeping _____ Weight _____ Pulse/Waking _____ Rising _____ Diff _____

Nutrition _____

_____

Distance ridden today _____ Workout type _____

Course _____

_____

_____ Weather _____

Remarks _____

_____

_____

_____

Wednesday _____

Hrs. Sleeping _____ Weight _____ Pulse/Waking _____ Rising _____ Diff _____

Nutrition _____

_____

Distance ridden today _____ Workout type _____

Course _____

_____

_____ Weather _____

Remarks _____

_____

_____

_____

'The bicycle tracks perfectly,
hands-off, only if loaned to
other, cleverer riders.'

Thursday _____
Hrs. Sleeping _____ Weight _____ Pulse/Waking _____ Rising _____ Diff _____
Nutrition _____
_____

Distance ridden today _____ Workout type _____
Course _____
_____
_____ Weather _____
Remarks _____
_____
_____
_____

Friday _____
Hrs. Sleeping _____ Weight _____ Pulse/Waking _____ Rising _____ Diff _____
Nutrition _____
_____

Distance ridden today _____ Workout type _____
Course _____
_____
_____ Weather _____
Remarks _____
_____
_____
_____

TGI Fridays time trial team in the 1993 Idaho Women's Challenge.

Saturday _____

Hrs. Sleeping _____ Weight _____ Pulse/Waking _____ Rising _____ Diff _____

Nutrition _____

_____

Distance ridden today _____ Workout type _____

Course _____

_____ Weather _____

Remarks _____

_____

_____

_____

Sunday _____

Hrs. Sleeping _____ Weight _____ Pulse/Waking _____ Rising _____ Diff _____

Nutrition _____

_____

Distance ridden today _____ Workout type _____

Course _____

_____ Weather _____

Remarks _____

_____

_____

_____

Race

Date _____ Time of Start _____ Event _____

Distance _____ Category ridden _____

Placing _____ Time _____

Competition _____

_____

Weather _____

Equipment _____

_____

Remarks _____

_____

_____

Weekly Summary

Distance this week _____

Mechanical notes _____

_____

_____

_____

Remarks _____

_____

_____

_____

_____

Week of _____

Monday _____

Hrs. Sleeping _____ Weight _____ Pulse/Waking _____ Rising _____ Diff _____

Nutrition _____
_____

Distance ridden today _____ Workout type _____

Course _____
_____

_____ Weather _____

Remarks _____
_____
_____
_____

Tuesday _____

Hrs. Sleeping _____ Weight _____ Pulse/Waking _____ Rising _____ Diff _____

Nutrition _____
_____

Distance ridden today _____ Workout type _____

Course _____
_____

_____ Weather _____

Remarks _____
_____
_____
_____

Wednesday _____

Hrs. Sleeping _____ Weight _____ Pulse/Waking _____ Rising _____ Diff _____

Nutrition _____
_____

Distance ridden today _____ Workout type _____

Course _____
_____

_____ Weather _____

Remarks _____
_____
_____
_____

Thursday _____

Hrs. Sleeping _____ Weight _____ Pulse/Waking _____ Rising _____ Diff _____
Nutrition _____
_____

Distance ridden today _____ Workout type _____
Course _____
_____
_____ Weather _____
Remarks _____
_____
_____
_____

Friday _____

Hrs. Sleeping _____ Weight _____ Pulse/Waking _____ Rising _____ Diff _____
Nutrition _____
_____

Distance ridden today _____ Workout type _____
Course _____
_____
_____ Weather _____
Remarks _____
_____
_____

Saturday _____

Hrs. Sleeping _____ Weight _____ Pulse/Waking _____ Rising _____ Diff _____
Nutrition _____
_____

Distance ridden today _____ Workout type _____
Course _____
_____
_____ Weather _____
Remarks _____
_____
_____

Sunday _____

Hrs. Sleeping _____ Weight _____ Pulse/Waking _____ Rising _____ Diff _____

Nutrition _____
_____

Distance ridden today _____ Workout type _____

Course _____
_____

_____ Weather _____

Remarks _____
_____
_____
_____

Race

Date _____ Time of Start _____ Event _____

Distance _____ Category ridden _____

Placing _____ Time _____

Competition _____
_____

Weather _____

Equipment _____
_____

Remarks _____
_____
_____

Weekly Summary

Distance this week _____

Mechanical notes _____
_____
_____
_____

Remarks _____
_____
_____
_____
_____
_____

Week of _____

Monday _____

Hrs. Sleeping _____ Weight _____ Pulse/Waking _____ Rising _____ Diff _____

Nutrition _____

_____

Distance ridden today _____ Workout type _____

Course _____

_____

_____ Weather _____

Remarks _____

_____

_____

_____

Tuesday _____

Hrs. Sleeping _____ Weight _____ Pulse/Waking _____ Rising _____ Diff _____

Nutrition _____

_____

Distance ridden today _____ Workout type _____

Course _____

_____

_____ Weather _____

Remarks _____

_____

_____

_____

Wednesday _____

Hrs. Sleeping _____ Weight _____ Pulse/Waking _____ Rising _____ Diff _____

Nutrition _____

_____

Distance ridden today _____ Workout type _____

Course _____

_____

_____ Weather _____

Remarks _____

_____

_____

_____

Thursday _____

Hrs. Sleeping _____ Weight _____ Pulse/Waking _____ Rising _____ Diff _____

Nutrition _____
_____

Distance ridden today _____ Workout type _____

Course _____
_____

_____ Weather _____

Remarks _____
_____
_____
_____

Friday _____

Hrs. Sleeping _____ Weight _____ Pulse/Waking _____ Rising _____ Diff _____

Nutrition _____
_____

Distance ridden today _____ Workout type _____

Course _____
_____

_____ Weather _____

Remarks _____
_____
_____
_____

Saturday _____

Hrs. Sleeping _____ Weight _____ Pulse/Waking _____ Rising _____ Diff _____

Nutrition _____
_____

Distance ridden today _____ Workout type _____

Course _____
_____

_____ Weather _____

Remarks _____
_____
_____
_____

Sunday _____

Hrs. Sleeping _____ Weight _____ Pulse/Waking _____ Rising _____ Diff _____

Nutrition _____

_____

Distance ridden today _____ Workout type _____

Course _____

_____ Weather _____

Remarks _____

_____

_____

_____

Race

Date _____ Time of Start _____ Event _____

Distance _____ Category ridden _____

Placing _____ Time _____

Competition _____

_____

Weather _____

Equipment _____

_____

Remarks _____

_____

_____

Weekly Summary

Distance this week _____

Mechanical notes _____

_____

_____

_____

Remarks _____

_____

_____

_____

_____

_____

Week of _____

Monday _____
Hrs. Sleeping _____ Weight _____ Pulse/Waking _____ Rising _____ Diff _____
Nutrition _____
_____
Distance ridden today _____ Workout type _____
Course _____
_____
_____ Weather _____
Remarks _____
_____
_____
_____

Tuesday _____
Hrs. Sleeping _____ Weight _____ Pulse/Waking _____ Rising _____ Diff _____
Nutrition _____
_____
Distance ridden today _____ Workout type _____
Course _____
_____
_____ Weather _____
Remarks _____
_____
_____
_____

Wednesday _____
Hrs. Sleeping _____ Weight _____ Pulse/Waking _____ Rising _____ Diff _____
Nutrition _____
_____
Distance ridden today _____ Workout type _____
Course _____
_____
_____ Weather _____
Remarks _____
_____
_____
_____

Thursday _____

Hrs. Sleeping _____ Weight _____ Pulse/Waking _____ Rising _____ Diff _____
Nutrition _____
_____

Distance ridden today _____ Workout type _____
Course _____
_____
_____ Weather _____
Remarks _____
_____
_____
_____

Friday _____

Hrs. Sleeping _____ Weight _____ Pulse/Waking _____ Rising _____ Diff _____
Nutrition _____
_____

Distance ridden today _____ Workout type _____
Course _____
_____
_____ Weather _____
Remarks _____
_____
_____

Saturday _____

Hrs. Sleeping _____ Weight _____ Pulse/Waking _____ Rising _____ Diff _____
Nutrition _____
_____

Distance ridden today _____ Workout type _____
Course _____
_____
_____ Weather _____
Remarks _____
_____
_____

Sunday _____

Hrs. Sleeping _____ Weight _____ Pulse/Waking _____ Rising _____ Diff _____

Nutrition _____

_____

Distance ridden today _____ Workout type _____

Course _____

_____

_____ Weather _____

Remarks _____

_____

_____

_____

Race

Date _____ Time of Start _____ Event _____

Distance _____ Category ridden _____

Placing _____ Time _____

Competition _____

_____

Weather _____

Equipment _____

_____

Remarks _____

_____

_____

Weekly Summary

Distance this week _____

Mechanical notes _____

_____

_____

_____

Remarks _____

_____

_____

_____

_____

_____

Week of _____

Monday _____

Hrs. Sleeping _____ Weight _____ Pulse/Waking _____ Rising _____ Diff _____

Nutrition _____

_____

Distance ridden today _____ Workout type _____

Course _____

_____

_____ Weather _____

Remarks _____

_____

_____

_____

Tuesday _____

Hrs. Sleeping _____ Weight _____ Pulse/Waking _____ Rising _____ Diff _____

Nutrition _____

_____

Distance ridden today _____ Workout type _____

Course _____ _____

_____

_____ Weather _____

Remarks _____

_____

_____

_____

Wednesday _____

Hrs. Sleeping _____ Weight _____ Pulse/Waking _____ Rising _____ Diff _____

Nutrition _____

_____

Distance ridden today _____ Workout type _____

Course _____

_____

_____ Weather _____

Remarks _____

_____

_____

_____

Thursday _____

Hrs. Sleeping _____ Weight _____ Pulse/Waking _____ Rising _____ Diff _____

Nutrition _____

_____

Distance ridden today _____ Workout type _____

Course _____

_____

_____ Weather _____

Remarks _____

_____

_____

_____

Friday _____

Hrs. Sleeping _____ Weight _____ Pulse/Waking _____ Rising _____ Diff _____

Nutrition _____

_____

Distance ridden today _____ Workout type _____

Course _____

_____

_____ Weather _____

Remarks _____

_____

_____

_____

Saturday _____

Hrs. Sleeping _____ Weight _____ Pulse/Waking _____ Rising _____ Diff _____

Nutrition _____

_____

Distance ridden today _____ Workout type _____

Course _____

_____

_____ Weather _____

Remarks _____

_____

_____

_____

Sunday _____

Hrs. Sleeping _____ Weight _____ Pulse/Waking _____ Rising _____ Diff _____

Nutrition _____

_____

Distance ridden today _____ Workout type _____

Course _____

_____

_____ Weather _____

Remarks _____

_____

_____

_____

Race

Date _____ Time of Start _____ Event _____

Distance _____ Category ridden _____

Placing _____ Time _____

Competition _____

_____

Weather _____

Equipment _____

_____

Remarks _____

_____

_____

Weekly Summary

Distance this week _____

Mechanical notes _____

_____

_____

_____

Remarks _____

_____

_____

_____

_____

_____

Week of _____

Monday _____
Hrs. Sleeping _____ Weight _____ Pulse/Waking _____ Rising _____ Diff _____
Nutrition _____
_____

Distance ridden today _____ Workout type _____
Course _____
_____
_____ Weather _____
Remarks _____
_____
_____
_____

Tuesday _____
Hrs. Sleeping _____ Weight _____ Pulse/Waking _____ Rising _____ Diff _____
Nutrition _____
_____

Distance ridden today _____ Workout type _____
Course _____
_____
_____ Weather _____
Remarks _____
_____
_____
_____

Wednesday _____
Hrs. Sleeping _____ Weight _____ Pulse/Waking _____ Rising _____ Diff _____
Nutrition _____
_____

Distance ridden today _____ Workout type _____
Course _____
_____
_____ Weather _____
Remarks _____
_____
_____
_____

Thursday _____
Hrs. Sleeping _____ Weight _____ Pulse/Waking _____ Rising _____ Diff _____
Nutrition _____

Distance ridden today _____ Workout type _____
Course _____
_____
_____ Weather _____
Remarks _____
_____
_____
_____

'He taught me to save energy,
to relax when I could
so I'd have something in reserve
for the crunches.'

Friday _____
Hrs. Sleeping _____ Weight _____ Pulse/Waking _____ Rising _____ Diff _____
Nutrition _____

Distance ridden today _____ Workout type _____
Course _____
_____
_____ Weather _____
Remarks _____
_____
_____
_____

Prologue time trial of 1992 Celestial Seasonings race in Boulder, Colorado.

Saturday _____

Hrs. Sleeping _____ Weight _____ Pulse/Waking _____ Rising _____ Diff _____

Nutrition _____

_____

Distance ridden today _____ Workout type _____

Course _____

_____

_____ Weather _____

Remarks _____

_____

_____

_____

Sunday _____

Hrs. Sleeping _____ Weight _____ Pulse/Waking _____ Rising _____ Diff _____

Nutrition _____

_____

Distance ridden today _____ Workout type _____

Course _____

_____

_____ Weather _____

Remarks _____

_____

_____

_____

Race

Date _____ Time of Start _____ Event _____

Distance _____ Category ridden _____

Placing_____ Time _____

Competition _____

_____

Weather _____

Equipment_____

_____

Remarks _____

_____

_____

Weekly Summary

Distance this week _____

Mechanical notes _____

_____

_____

_____

Remarks_____

_____

_____

_____

_____

_____

Week of _____

Monday _____

Hrs. Sleeping _____ Weight _____ Pulse/Waking _____ Rising _____ Diff _____
Nutrition _____
_____

Distance ridden today _____ Workout type _____
Course _____
_____
_____ Weather _____
Remarks _____
_____
_____
_____

Tuesday _____

Hrs. Sleeping _____ Weight _____ Pulse/Waking _____ Rising _____ Diff _____
Nutrition _____
_____

Distance ridden today _____ Workout type _____
Course _____
_____
_____ Weather _____
Remarks _____
_____
_____
_____

Wednesday _____

Hrs. Sleeping _____ Weight _____ Pulse/Waking _____ Rising _____ Diff _____
Nutrition _____
_____

Distance ridden today _____ Workout type _____
Course _____
_____
_____ Weather _____
Remarks _____
_____
_____
_____

Thursday _____

Hrs. Sleeping _____ Weight _____ Pulse/Waking _____ Rising _____ Diff _____

Nutrition _____

_____

Distance ridden today _____ Workout type _____

Course _____

_____

_____ Weather _____

Remarks _____

_____

_____

_____

Friday _____

Hrs. Sleeping _____ Weight _____ Pulse/Waking _____ Rising _____ Diff _____

Nutrition _____

_____

Distance ridden today _____ Workout type _____

Course _____

_____

_____ Weather _____

Remarks _____

_____

_____

_____

Saturday _____

Hrs. Sleeping _____ Weight _____ Pulse/Waking _____ Rising _____ Diff _____

Nutrition _____

_____

Distance ridden today _____ Workout type _____

Course _____

_____

_____ Weather _____

Remarks _____

_____

_____

_____

Sunday _____

Hrs. Sleeping _____ Weight _____ Pulse/Waking _____ Rising _____ Diff _____

Nutrition _____

_____

Distance ridden today _____ Workout type _____

Course _____

_____

_____ Weather _____

Remarks _____

_____

_____

_____

Race

Date _____ Time of Start _____ Event _____

Distance _____ Category ridden _____

Placing_____ Time _____

Competition _____

_____

Weather_____

Equipment_____

_____

Remarks_____

_____

_____

Weekly Summary

Distance this week _____

Mechanical notes _____

_____

_____

_____

Remarks_____

_____

_____

_____

_____

_____

Week of _____

Monday _____
Hrs. Sleeping _____ Weight _____ Pulse/Waking _____ Rising _____ Diff _____
Nutrition _____
_____

Distance ridden today _____ Workout type _____
Course _____
_____
_____ Weather _____
Remarks _____
_____
_____
_____

Tuesday _____
Hrs. Sleeping _____ Weight _____ Pulse/Waking _____ Rising _____ Diff _____
Nutrition _____
_____

Distance ridden today _____ Workout type _____
Course _____
_____
_____ Weather _____
Remarks _____
_____
_____
_____

Wednesday _____
Hrs. Sleeping _____ Weight _____ Pulse/Waking _____ Rising _____ Diff _____
Nutrition _____
_____

Distance ridden today _____ Workout type _____
Course _____
_____
_____ Weather _____
Remarks _____
_____
_____
_____

Thursday _____

Hrs. Sleeping _____ Weight _____ Pulse/Waking _____ Rising _____ Diff _____

Nutrition _____

_____

Distance ridden today _____ Workout type _____

Course _____

_____

_____ Weather _____

Remarks _____

_____

_____

_____

Friday _____

Hrs. Sleeping _____ Weight _____ Pulse/Waking _____ Rising _____ Diff _____

Nutrition _____

_____

Distance ridden today _____ Workout type _____

Course _____

_____

_____ Weather _____

Remarks _____

_____

_____

Saturday _____

Hrs. Sleeping _____ Weight _____ Pulse/Waking _____ Rising _____ Diff _____

Nutrition _____

_____

Distance ridden today _____ Workout type _____

Course _____

_____

_____ Weather _____

Remarks _____

_____

_____

Sunday _____

Hrs. Sleeping _____ Weight _____ Pulse/Waking _____ Rising _____ Diff _____

Nutrition _____

_____

Distance ridden today _____ Workout type _____

Course _____

_____

_____ Weather _____

Remarks _____

_____

_____

_____

Race

Date _____ Time of Start _____ Event _____

Distance _____ Category ridden _____

Placing _____ Time _____

Competition _____

_____

Weather _____

Equipment _____

_____

Remarks _____

_____

_____

Weekly Summary

Distance this week _____

Mechanical notes _____

_____

_____

_____

Remarks _____

_____

_____

_____

_____

_____

Week of _____

Monday _____
Hrs. Sleeping _____ Weight _____ Pulse/Waking _____ Rising _____ Diff _____
Nutrition _____
_____

Distance ridden today _____ Workout type _____
Course _____
_____
_____ Weather _____
Remarks _____
_____
_____
_____

Tuesday _____
Hrs. Sleeping _____ Weight _____ Pulse/Waking _____ Rising _____ Diff _____
Nutrition _____
_____

Distance ridden today _____ Workout type _____
Course _____
_____
_____ Weather _____
Remarks _____
_____
_____
_____

Wednesday _____
Hrs. Sleeping _____ Weight _____ Pulse/Waking _____ Rising _____ Diff _____
Nutrition _____
_____

Distance ridden today _____ Workout type _____
Course _____
_____
_____ Weather _____
Remarks _____
_____
_____
_____

> *'He'd heat a pan of grease*
> *on the stove to soak his chain.*
> *The house smelled so bad*
> *their old cat left for good.'*

Thursday _____

Hrs. Sleeping _____ Weight _____ Pulse/Waking _____ Rising _____ Diff _____

Nutrition _____

_____

Distance ridden today _____ Workout type _____

Course _____

_____

_____ Weather _____

Remarks _____

_____

_____

_____

Friday _____

Hrs. Sleeping _____ Weight _____ Pulse/Waking _____ Rising _____ Diff _____

Nutrition _____

_____

Distance ridden today _____ Workout type _____

Course _____

_____ Weather _____

Remarks _____

_____

_____

_____

1990 Ruta Mexico.

Saturday ────────────────

Hrs. Sleeping _____ Weight _____ Pulse/Waking _____ Rising _____ Diff _____

Nutrition _____

_____

Distance ridden today _____ Workout type _____

Course _____

_____

_____ Weather _____

Remarks _____

_____

_____

_____

Sunday _____

Hrs. Sleeping _____ Weight _____ Pulse/Waking _____ Rising _____ Diff _____

Nutrition _____

_____

Distance ridden today _____ Workout type _____

Course _____

_____

_____ Weather _____

Remarks _____

_____

_____

_____

Race

Date _____ Time of Start _____ Event _____

Distance _____ Category ridden _____

Placing _____ Time _____

Competition _____

_____

Weather _____

Equipment _____

_____

Remarks _____

_____

_____

Weekly Summary

Distance this week _____

Mechanical notes _____

_____

_____

_____

Remarks _____

_____

_____

_____

_____

_____

Week of _____

Monday _____
Hrs. Sleeping _____ Weight _____ Pulse/Waking _____ Rising _____ Diff _____
Nutrition _____
_____
Distance ridden today _____ Workout type _____
Course _____
_____
_____ Weather _____
Remarks _____
_____
_____
_____

Tuesday _____
Hrs. Sleeping _____ Weight _____ Pulse/Waking _____ Rising _____ Diff _____
Nutrition _____
_____
Distance ridden today _____ Workout type _____
Course _____
_____
_____ Weather _____
Remarks _____
_____
_____
_____

Wednesday _____
Hrs. Sleeping _____ Weight _____ Pulse/Waking _____ Rising _____ Diff _____
Nutrition _____
_____
Distance ridden today _____ Workout type _____
Course _____
_____
_____ Weather _____
Remarks _____
_____
_____
_____

Thursday _____

Hrs. Sleeping _____ Weight _____ Pulse/Waking _____ Rising _____ Diff _____

Nutrition _____

_____

Distance ridden today _____ Workout type _____

Course _____

_____

_____ Weather _____

Remarks _____

_____

_____

_____

Friday _____

Hrs. Sleeping _____ Weight _____ Pulse/Waking _____ Rising _____ Diff _____

Nutrition _____

_____

Distance ridden today _____ Workout type _____

Course _____

_____

_____ Weather _____

Remarks _____

_____

_____

_____

Saturday _____

Hrs. Sleeping _____ Weight _____ Pulse/Waking _____ Rising _____ Diff _____

Nutrition _____

_____

Distance ridden today _____ Workout type _____

Course _____

_____

_____ Weather _____

Remarks _____

_____

_____

_____

Sunday _____

Hrs. Sleeping _____ Weight _____ Pulse/Waking _____ Rising _____ Diff _____

Nutrition _____

_____

Distance ridden today _____ Workout type _____

Course _____

_____

_____ Weather _____

Remarks _____

_____

_____

_____

Race

Date _____ Time of Start _____ Event _____

Distance _____ Category ridden _____

Placing_____ Time _____

Competition _____

_____

Weather_____

Equipment_____

_____

Remarks_____

_____

_____

Weekly Summary

Distance this week _____

Mechanical notes _____

_____

_____

_____

Remarks_____

_____

_____

_____

_____

Week of _____

Monday _____
Hrs. Sleeping _____ Weight _____ Pulse/Waking _____ Rising _____ Diff _____
Nutrition _____
_____

Distance ridden today _____ Workout type _____
Course _____
_____
_____ Weather _____
Remarks _____
_____
_____
_____

Tuesday _____
Hrs. Sleeping _____ Weight _____ Pulse/Waking _____ Rising _____ Diff _____
Nutrition _____
_____

Distance ridden today _____ Workout type _____
Course _____
_____
_____ Weather _____
Remarks _____
_____
_____
_____

Wednesday _____
Hrs. Sleeping _____ Weight _____ Pulse/Waking _____ Rising _____ Diff _____
Nutrition _____
_____

Distance ridden today _____ Workout type _____
Course _____
_____
_____ Weather _____
Remarks _____
_____
_____
_____

Thursday _____

Hrs. Sleeping _____ Weight _____ Pulse/Waking _____ Rising _____ Diff _____

Nutrition _____

_____

Distance ridden today _____ Workout type _____

Course _____

_____

_____ Weather _____

Remarks _____

_____

_____

_____

Friday _____

Hrs. Sleeping _____ Weight _____ Pulse/Waking _____ Rising _____ Diff _____

Nutrition _____

_____

Distance ridden today _____ Workout type _____

Course _____

_____

_____ Weather _____

Remarks _____

_____

_____

_____

Saturday _____

Hrs. Sleeping _____ Weight _____ Pulse/Waking _____ Rising _____ Diff _____

Nutrition _____

_____

Distance ridden today _____ Workout type _____

Course _____

_____

_____ Weather _____

Remarks _____

_____

_____

_____

Sunday _____

Hrs. Sleeping _____ Weight _____ Pulse/Waking _____ Rising _____ Diff _____

Nutrition _____

Distance ridden today _____ Workout type _____

Course _____

_____ Weather _____

Remarks _____

Race

Date _____ Time of Start _____ Event _____

Distance _____ Category ridden _____

Placing _____ Time _____

Competition _____

Weather _____

Equipment _____

Remarks _____

Weekly Summary

Distance this week _____

Mechanical notes _____

Remarks _____

Week of _____

Monday _____

Hrs. Sleeping _____ Weight _____ Pulse/Waking _____ Rising _____ Diff _____

Nutrition _____
_____

Distance ridden today _____ Workout type _____
Course _____
_____
_____ Weather _____
Remarks _____
_____
_____
_____

Tuesday _____

Hrs. Sleeping _____ Weight _____ Pulse/Waking _____ Rising _____ Diff _____

Nutrition _____
_____

Distance ridden today _____ Workout type _____
Course _____
_____
_____ Weather _____
Remarks _____
_____
_____
_____

Wednesday _____

Hrs. Sleeping _____ Weight _____ Pulse/Waking _____ Rising _____ Diff _____

Nutrition _____
_____

Distance ridden today _____ Workout type _____
Course _____
_____
_____ Weather _____
Remarks _____
_____
_____
_____

Thursday _____

Hrs. Sleeping _____ Weight _____ Pulse/Waking _____ Rising _____ Diff _____

Nutrition _____

_____

Distance ridden today _____ Workout type _____

Course _____

_____

_____ Weather _____

Remarks _____

_____

_____

_____

Friday _____

Hrs. Sleeping _____ Weight _____ Pulse/Waking _____ Rising _____ Diff _____

Nutrition _____

_____

Distance ridden today _____ Workout type _____

Course _____

_____

_____ Weather _____

Remarks _____

_____

_____

_____

Saturday _____

Hrs. Sleeping _____ Weight _____ Pulse/Waking _____ Rising _____ Diff _____

Nutrition _____

_____

Distance ridden today _____ Workout type _____

Course _____

_____

_____ Weather _____

Remarks _____

_____

_____

_____

Sunday _____

Hrs. Sleeping _____ Weight _____ Pulse/Waking _____ Rising ____ Diff _____
Nutrition _____
_____

Distance ridden today _____ Workout type _____
Course _____
_____
_____ Weather _____
Remarks _____
_____
_____
_____

Race

Date _____ Time of Start _____ Event _____
Distance _____ Category ridden _____
Placing _____ Time _____
Competition _____
_____
Weather _____
Equipment _____
_____
Remarks _____
_____
_____

Weekly Summary

Distance this week _____
Mechanical notes _____
_____
_____
_____
Remarks _____
_____
_____
_____
_____
_____

Week of _____

Monday _____
Hrs. Sleeping _____ Weight _____ Pulse/Waking _____ Rising _____ Diff _____
Nutrition _____
_____
Distance ridden today _____ Workout type _____
Course _____
_____
_____ Weather _____
Remarks _____
_____
_____
_____

Tuesday _____
Hrs. Sleeping _____ Weight _____ Pulse/Waking _____ Rising _____ Diff _____
Nutrition _____
_____
Distance ridden today _____ Workout type _____
Course _____
_____
_____ Weather _____
Remarks _____
_____
_____
_____

Wednesday _____
Hrs. Sleeping _____ Weight _____ Pulse/Waking _____ Rising _____ Diff _____
Nutrition _____
_____
Distance ridden today _____ Workout type _____
Course _____
_____
_____ Weather _____
Remarks _____
_____
_____
_____

Thursday _____

Hrs. Sleeping _____ Weight _____ Pulse/Waking _____ Rising _____ Diff _____

Nutrition _____

_____

Distance ridden today _____ Workout type _____

Course _____

_____

_____ Weather _____

Remarks _____

_____

_____

_____

Friday _____

Hrs. Sleeping _____ Weight _____ Pulse/Waking _____ Rising _____ Diff _____

Nutrition _____

_____

Distance ridden today _____ Workout type _____

Course _____

_____

_____ Weather _____

Remarks _____

_____

_____

_____

Saturday _____

Hrs. Sleeping _____ Weight _____ Pulse/Waking _____ Rising _____ Diff _____

Nutrition _____

_____

Distance ridden today _____ Workout type _____

Course _____

_____

_____ Weather _____

Remarks _____

_____

_____

_____

Sunday _____

Hrs. Sleeping _____ Weight _____ Pulse/Waking _____ Rising _____ Diff _____

Nutrition _____

_____

Distance ridden today _____ Workout type _____

Course _____

_____

_____ Weather _____

Remarks _____

_____

_____

_____

Race

Date _____ Time of Start _____ Event _____

Distance _____ Category ridden _____

Placing _____ Time _____

Competition _____

_____

Weather _____

Equipment _____

_____

Remarks _____

_____

_____

Weekly Summary

Distance this week _____

Mechanical notes _____

_____

_____

_____

Remarks _____

_____

_____

_____

_____

_____

Week of _____

Monday _____

Hrs. Sleeping _____ Weight _____ Pulse/Waking _____ Rising _____ Diff _____

Nutrition _____

_____

Distance ridden today _____ Workout type _____

Course _____

_____

_____ Weather _____

Remarks _____

_____

_____

_____

Tuesday _____

Hrs. Sleeping _____ Weight _____ Pulse/Waking _____ Rising _____ Diff _____

Nutrition _____

_____

Distance ridden today _____ Workout type _____

Course _____

_____

_____ Weather _____

Remarks _____

_____

_____

_____

Wednesday _____

Hrs. Sleeping _____ Weight _____ Pulse/Waking _____ Rising _____ Diff _____

Nutrition _____

_____

Distance ridden today _____ Workout type _____

Course _____

_____

_____ Weather _____

Remarks _____

_____

_____

_____

Thursday _____

Hrs. Sleeping _____ Weight _____ Pulse/Waking _____ Rising _____ Diff _____

Nutrition _____

_____

Distance ridden today _____ Workout type _____

Course _____

_____

_____ Weather _____

Remarks _____

_____

_____

_____

*'Soon they learned that peer approval
came from a quiet display of
pack-riding skills,
not head-down, big-gear showboating.'*

Friday _____

Hrs. Sleeping _____ Weight _____ Pulse/Waking _____ Rising _____ Diff _____

Nutrition _____

_____

Distance ridden today _____ Workout type _____

Course _____

_____

_____ Weather _____

Remarks _____

_____

_____

_____

Saturn rider Scott Fortner time trials at 1993 Vuelta de Bisbee, Arizona.

Saturday _____

Hrs. Sleeping _____ Weight _____ Pulse/Waking _____ Rising _____ Diff _____

Nutrition _____

_____

Distance ridden today _____ Workout type _____

Course _____

_____

_____ Weather _____

Remarks _____

_____

_____

_____

Sunday _____

Hrs. Sleeping _____ Weight _____ Pulse/Waking _____ Rising _____ Diff _____

Nutrition _____

_____

Distance ridden today _____ Workout type _____

Course _____

_____

_____ Weather _____

Remarks _____

_____

_____

_____

Race

Date _____ Time of Start _____ Event _____

Distance _____ Category ridden _____

Placing _____ Time _____

Competition _____

_____

Weather _____

Equipment _____

_____

Remarks _____

_____

_____

Weekly Summary

Distance this week _____

Mechanical notes _____

_____

_____

Remarks _____

_____

_____

_____

_____

_____

Week of _____

Monday _____

Hrs. Sleeping _____ Weight _____ Pulse/Waking _____ Rising _____ Diff _____

Nutrition _____

_____

Distance ridden today _____ Workout type _____

Course _____

_____

_____ Weather _____

Remarks _____

_____

_____

_____

Tuesday _____

Hrs. Sleeping _____ Weight _____ Pulse/Waking _____ Rising _____ Diff _____

Nutrition _____

_____

Distance ridden today _____ Workout type _____

Course _____

_____

_____ Weather _____

Remarks _____

_____

_____

_____

Wednesday _____

Hrs. Sleeping _____ Weight _____ Pulse/Waking _____ Rising _____ Diff _____

Nutrition _____

_____

Distance ridden today _____ Workout type _____

Course _____

_____

_____ Weather _____

Remarks _____

_____

_____

_____

Thursday _____

Hrs. Sleeping _____ Weight _____ Pulse/Waking _____ Rising _____ Diff _____

Nutrition _____

_____

Distance ridden today _____ Workout type _____

Course _____

_____

_____ Weather _____

Remarks _____

_____

_____

_____

Friday _____

Hrs. Sleeping _____ Weight _____ Pulse/Waking _____ Rising _____ Diff _____

Nutrition _____

_____

Distance ridden today _____ Workout type _____

Course _____

_____

_____ Weather _____

Remarks _____

_____

_____

_____

Saturday _____

Hrs. Sleeping _____ Weight _____ Pulse/Waking _____ Rising _____ Diff _____

Nutrition _____

_____

Distance ridden today _____ Workout type _____

Course _____

_____

_____ Weather _____

Remarks _____

_____

_____

_____

Sunday _____

Hrs. Sleeping _____ Weight _____ Pulse/Waking _____ Rising _____ Diff _____

Nutrition _____

_____

Distance ridden today _____ Workout type _____

Course _____

_____

_____ Weather _____

Remarks _____

_____

_____

_____

Race

Date _____ Time of Start _____ Event _____

Distance _____ Category ridden _____

Placing _____ Time _____

Competition _____

_____

Weather _____

Equipment _____

_____

Remarks _____

_____

_____

Weekly Summary

Distance this week _____

Mechanical notes _____

_____

_____

_____

Remarks _____

_____

_____

_____

_____

_____

Week of _____

Monday _____

Hrs. Sleeping _____ Weight _____ Pulse/Waking _____ Rising _____ Diff _____

Nutrition _____

_____

Distance ridden today _____ Workout type _____

Course _____

_____

_____ Weather _____

Remarks _____

_____

_____

_____

Tuesday _____

Hrs. Sleeping _____ Weight _____ Pulse/Waking _____ Rising _____ Diff _____

Nutrition _____

_____

Distance ridden today _____ Workout type _____

Course _____

_____

_____ Weather _____

Remarks _____

_____

_____

_____

Wednesday _____

Hrs. Sleeping _____ Weight _____ Pulse/Waking _____ Rising _____ Diff _____

Nutrition _____

_____

Distance ridden today _____ Workout type _____

Course _____

_____

_____ Weather _____

Remarks _____

_____

_____

_____

Thursday _____

Hrs. Sleeping _____ Weight _____ Pulse/Waking _____ Rising _____ Diff _____

Nutrition _____

_____

Distance ridden today _____ Workout type _____

Course _____

_____

_____ Weather _____

Remarks _____

_____

_____

_____

Friday _____

Hrs. Sleeping _____ Weight _____ Pulse/Waking _____ Rising _____ Diff _____

Nutrition _____

_____

Distance ridden today _____ Workout type _____

Course _____

_____

_____ Weather _____

Remarks _____

_____

_____

_____

Saturday _____

Hrs. Sleeping _____ Weight _____ Pulse/Waking _____ Rising _____ Diff _____

Nutrition _____

_____

Distance ridden today _____ Workout type _____

Course _____

_____

_____ Weather _____

Remarks _____

_____

_____

_____

Sunday _____

Hrs. Sleeping _____ Weight _____ Pulse/Waking _____ Rising _____ Diff _____

Nutrition _____

_____

Distance ridden today _____ Workout type _____

Course _____

_____

_____ Weather _____

Remarks _____

_____

_____

_____

Race

Date _____ Time of Start _____ Event _____

Distance _____ Category ridden _____

Placing _____ Time _____

Competition _____

_____

Weather _____

Equipment _____

_____

Remarks _____

_____

_____

Weekly Summary

Distance this week _____

Mechanical notes _____

_____

_____

_____

Remarks _____

_____

_____

_____

_____

_____

Week of _____

Monday _____

Hrs. Sleeping _____ Weight _____ Pulse/Waking _____ Rising _____ Diff _____

Nutrition _____

_____

Distance ridden today _____ Workout type _____

Course _____

_____

_____ Weather _____

Remarks _____

_____

_____

_____

Tuesday _____

Hrs. Sleeping _____ Weight _____ Pulse/Waking _____ Rising _____ Diff _____

Nutrition _____

_____

Distance ridden today _____ Workout type _____

Course _____

_____

_____ Weather _____

Remarks _____

_____

_____

_____

Wednesday _____

Hrs. Sleeping _____ Weight _____ Pulse/Waking _____ Rising _____ Diff _____

Nutrition _____

_____

Distance ridden today _____ Workout type _____

Course _____

_____

_____ Weather _____

Remarks _____

_____

_____

_____

> *'When I bought my frame,*
> *I felt sure it was identical*
> *to the one Giancarlo Guacamole*
> *rode in the Giro.'*

Thursday _____

Hrs. Sleeping _____ Weight _____ Pulse/Waking _____ Rising _____ Diff _____

Nutrition _____

_____

Distance ridden today _____ Workout type _____

Course _____

_____

_____ Weather _____

Remarks _____

_____

_____

_____

Friday _____

Hrs. Sleeping _____ Weight _____ Pulse/Waking _____ Rising _____ Diff _____

Nutrition _____

_____

Distance ridden today _____ Workout type _____

Course _____

_____

_____ Weather _____

Remarks _____

_____

_____

_____

World and National champion Eve Stephenson in the Vuelta de Bisbee, Arizona.

Saturday _____

Hrs. Sleeping _____ Weight _____ Pulse/Waking _____ Rising _____ Diff _____

Nutrition _____

_____

Distance ridden today _____ Workout type _____

Course _____

_____

_____ Weather _____

Remarks _____

_____

_____

_____

_____

Sunday _____

Hrs. Sleeping _____ Weight _____ Pulse/Waking _____ Rising _____ Diff _____

Nutrition _____

_____

Distance ridden today _____ Workout type _____

Course _____

_____

_____ Weather _____

Remarks _____

_____

_____

_____

Race

Date _____ Time of Start _____ Event _____

Distance _____ Category ridden _____

Placing _____ Time _____

Competition _____

_____

Weather _____

Equipment _____

_____

Remarks _____

_____

Weekly Summary

Distance this week _____

Mechanical notes _____

_____

_____

_____

Remarks _____

_____

_____

_____

_____

_____

Week of _____

Monday _____

Hrs. Sleeping _____ Weight _____ Pulse/Waking _____ Rising _____ Diff _____

Nutrition _____

_____

Distance ridden today _____ Workout type _____

Course _____

_____

_____ Weather _____

Remarks _____

_____

_____

_____

Tuesday _____

Hrs. Sleeping _____ Weight _____ Pulse/Waking _____ Rising _____ Diff _____

Nutrition _____

_____

Distance ridden today _____ Workout type _____

Course _____

_____

_____ Weather _____

Remarks _____

_____

_____

_____

Wednesday _____

Hrs. Sleeping _____ Weight _____ Pulse/Waking _____ Rising _____ Diff _____

Nutrition _____

_____

Distance ridden today _____ Workout type _____

Course _____

_____

_____ Weather _____

Remarks _____

_____

_____

_____

Thursday _____

Hrs. Sleeping _____ Weight _____ Pulse/Waking _____ Rising _____ Diff _____

Nutrition _____

_____

Distance ridden today _____ Workout type _____

Course _____

_____

_____ Weather _____

Remarks _____

_____

_____

_____

Friday _____

Hrs. Sleeping _____ Weight _____ Pulse/Waking _____ Rising _____ Diff _____

Nutrition _____

_____

Distance ridden today _____ Workout type _____

Course _____

_____

_____ Weather _____

Remarks _____

_____

_____

_____

Saturday _____

Hrs. Sleeping _____ Weight _____ Pulse/Waking _____ Rising _____ Diff _____

Nutrition _____

_____

Distance ridden today _____ Workout type _____

Course _____

_____

_____ Weather _____

Remarks _____

_____

_____

_____

Sunday _____

Hrs. Sleeping _____ Weight _____ Pulse/Waking _____ Rising _____ Diff _____

Nutrition _____

_____

Distance ridden today _____ Workout type _____

Course _____

_____

_____ Weather _____

Remarks _____

_____

_____

_____

Race

Date _____ Time of Start _____ Event _____

Distance _____ Category ridden _____

Placing _____ Time _____

Competition _____

_____

Weather _____

Equipment _____

_____

Remarks _____

_____

_____

Weekly Summary

Distance this week _____

Mechanical notes _____

_____

_____

_____

Remarks _____

_____

_____

_____

_____

Week of _____

Monday _____
Hrs. Sleeping _____ Weight _____ Pulse/Waking _____ Rising _____ Diff _____

Nutrition _____

_____

Distance ridden today _____ Workout type _____

Course _____

_____

_____ Weather _____

Remarks _____

_____

_____

_____

Tuesday _____
Hrs. Sleeping _____ Weight _____ Pulse/Waking _____ Rising _____ Diff _____

Nutrition _____

_____

Distance ridden today _____ Workout type _____

Course _____

_____

_____ Weather _____

Remarks _____

_____

_____

_____

Wednesday _____
Hrs. Sleeping _____ Weight _____ Pulse/Waking _____ Rising _____ Diff _____

Nutrition _____

_____

Distance ridden today _____ Workout type _____

Course _____

_____

_____ Weather _____

Remarks _____

_____

_____

_____

Thursday _____
Hrs. Sleeping _____ Weight _____ Pulse/Waking _____ Rising _____ Diff _____
Nutrition _____
_____

Distance ridden today _____ Workout type _____
Course _____
_____
_____ Weather _____
Remarks _____
_____
_____
_____

Friday _____
Hrs. Sleeping _____ Weight _____ Pulse/Waking _____ Rising _____ Diff _____
Nutrition _____
_____

Distance ridden today _____ Workout type _____
Course _____
_____
_____ Weather _____
Remarks _____
_____
_____
_____

Saturday _____
Hrs. Sleeping _____ Weight _____ Pulse/Waking _____ Rising _____ Diff _____
Nutrition _____
_____

Distance ridden today _____ Workout type _____
Course _____
_____
_____ Weather _____
Remarks _____
_____
_____
_____

Sunday _____

Hrs. Sleeping _____ Weight _____ Pulse/Waking _____ Rising _____ Diff _____

Nutrition _____

_____

Distance ridden today _____ Workout type _____

Course _____

_____

_____ Weather _____

Remarks _____

_____

_____

_____

Race

Date _____ Time of Start _____ Event _____

Distance _____ Category ridden _____

Placing _____ Time _____

Competition _____

_____

Weather _____

Equipment _____

_____

Remarks _____

_____

_____

Weekly Summary

Distance this week _____

Mechanical notes _____

_____

_____

_____

Remarks _____

_____

_____

_____

_____

_____

Week of _____

Monday _____
Hrs. Sleeping _____ Weight _____ Pulse/Waking _____ Rising _____ Diff _____
Nutrition _____
_____

Distance ridden today _____ Workout type _____
Course _____
_____
_____ Weather _____
Remarks _____
_____
_____
_____

Tuesday _____
Hrs. Sleeping _____ Weight _____ Pulse/Waking _____ Rising _____ Diff _____
Nutrition _____
_____

Distance ridden today _____ Workout type _____
Course _____
_____
_____ Weather _____
Remarks _____
_____
_____
_____

Wednesday _____
Hrs. Sleeping _____ Weight _____ Pulse/Waking _____ Rising _____ Diff _____
Nutrition _____
_____

Distance ridden today _____ Workout type _____
Course _____
_____
_____ Weather _____
Remarks _____
_____
_____
_____

Thursday _____

Hrs. Sleeping _____ Weight _____ Pulse/Waking _____ Rising _____ Diff _____

Nutrition _____

_____

Distance ridden today _____ Workout type _____

Course _____

_____

_____ Weather _____

Remarks _____

_____

_____

_____

Friday _____

Hrs. Sleeping _____ Weight _____ Pulse/Waking _____ Rising _____ Diff _____

Nutrition _____

_____

Distance ridden today _____ Workout type _____

Course _____

_____

_____ Weather _____

Remarks _____

_____

_____

Saturday _____

Hrs. Sleeping _____ Weight _____ Pulse/Waking _____ Rising _____ Diff _____

Nutrition _____

_____

Distance ridden today _____ Workout type _____

Course _____

_____

_____ Weather _____

Remarks _____

_____

_____

_____

Sunday _____

Hrs. Sleeping _____ Weight _____ Pulse/Waking _____ Rising _____ Diff _____

Nutrition _____
_____

Distance ridden today _____ Workout type _____

Course _____
_____
_____ Weather _____

Remarks _____
_____
_____
_____

Race

Date _____ Time of Start _____ Event _____

Distance _____ Category ridden _____

Placing _____ Time _____

Competition _____
_____

Weather _____

Equipment _____
_____

Remarks _____
_____
_____

Weekly Summary

Distance this week _____

Mechanical notes _____
_____
_____
_____

Remarks _____
_____
_____
_____
_____
_____

Week of _____

Monday _____

Hrs. Sleeping _____ Weight _____ Pulse/Waking _____ Rising _____ Diff _____

Nutrition _____

_____

Distance ridden today _____ Workout type _____

Course _____

_____

_____ Weather _____

Remarks _____

_____

_____

_____

Tuesday _____

Hrs. Sleeping _____ Weight _____ Pulse/Waking _____ Rising _____ Diff _____

Nutrition _____

_____

Distance ridden today _____ Workout type _____

Course _____

_____

_____ Weather _____

Remarks _____

_____

_____

_____

Wednesday _____

Hrs. Sleeping _____ Weight _____ Pulse/Waking _____ Rising _____ Diff _____

Nutrition _____

_____

Distance ridden today _____ Workout type _____

Course _____

_____

_____ Weather _____

Remarks _____

_____

_____

_____

Thursday _____

Hrs. Sleeping _____ Weight _____ Pulse/Waking _____ Rising _____ Diff _____

Nutrition _____

_____

Distance ridden today _____ Workout type _____

Course _____

_____

_____ Weather _____

Remarks _____

_____

_____

_____

Friday _____

Hrs. Sleeping _____ Weight _____ Pulse/Waking _____ Rising _____ Diff _____

Nutrition _____

_____

Distance ridden today _____ Workout type _____

Course _____

_____

_____ Weather _____

Remarks _____

_____

_____

_____

Saturday _____

Hrs. Sleeping _____ Weight _____ Pulse/Waking _____ Rising _____ Diff _____

Nutrition _____

_____

Distance ridden today _____ Workout type _____

Course _____

_____

_____ Weather _____

Remarks _____

_____

_____

_____

Sunday _____

Hrs. Sleeping _____ Weight _____ Pulse/Waking _____ Rising _____ Diff _____

Nutrition _____

_____

Distance ridden today _____ Workout type _____

Course _____

_____

_____ Weather _____

Remarks _____

_____

_____

_____

Race

Date _____ Time of Start _____ Event _____

Distance _____ Category ridden _____

Placing _____ Time _____

Competition _____

_____

Weather _____

Equipment _____

_____

Remarks _____

_____

_____

Weekly Summary

Distance this week _____

Mechanical notes _____

_____

_____

_____

Remarks _____

_____

_____

_____

_____

_____

Week of _____

Monday _____
Hrs. Sleeping _____ Weight _____ Pulse/Waking _____ Rising _____ Diff _____
Nutrition _____
_____
Distance ridden today _____ Workout type _____
Course _____
_____
_____ Weather _____
Remarks _____
_____
_____
_____

Tuesday _____
Hrs. Sleeping _____ Weight _____ Pulse/Waking _____ Rising _____ Diff _____
Nutrition _____
_____
Distance ridden today _____ Workout type _____
Course _____
_____
_____ Weather _____
Remarks _____
_____
_____
_____

Wednesday _____
Hrs. Sleeping _____ Weight _____ Pulse/Waking _____ Rising _____ Diff _____
Nutrition _____
_____
Distance ridden today _____ Workout type _____
Course _____
_____
_____ Weather _____
Remarks _____
_____
_____
_____

Thursday _____
Hrs. Sleeping _____ Weight _____ Pulse/Waking _____ Rising _____ Diff _____
Nutrition _____
_____

Distance ridden today _____ Workout type _____
Course _____
_____
_____ Weather _____
Remarks _____
_____
_____
_____

Friday _____
Hrs. Sleeping _____ Weight _____ Pulse/Waking _____ Rising _____ Diff _____
Nutrition _____
_____

Distance ridden today _____ Workout type _____
Course _____
_____
_____ Weather _____
Remarks _____
_____
_____
_____

'There are some things in life
that people have to do.
You have to pay taxes,
and you have to glue your tires.'

Saturday _____

Hrs. Sleeping _____ Weight _____ Pulse/Waking _____ Rising _____ Diff _____

Nutrition _____

_____

Distance ridden today _____ Workout type _____

Course _____

_____ Weather _____

Remarks _____

_____

_____

_____

Exeter road race in the 1993 Dole Classic, California.

Sunday _____

Hrs. Sleeping _____ Weight _____ Pulse/Waking _____ Rising _____ Diff _____

Nutrition _____

_____

Distance ridden today _____ Workout type _____

Course _____

_____

_____ Weather _____

Remarks _____

_____

_____

_____

Race

Date _____ Time of Start _____ Event _____

Distance _____ Category ridden _____

Placing_____ Time _____

Competition _____

_____

Weather _____

Equipment_____

_____

Remarks_____

_____

_____

Weekly Summary

Distance this week _____

Mechanical notes _____

_____

_____

_____

Remarks_____

_____

_____

_____

_____

_____

Week of _____

Monday _____
Hrs. Sleeping _____ Weight _____ Pulse/Waking _____ Rising ____ Diff _____
Nutrition _____
_____

Distance ridden today _____ Workout type _____
Course _____
_____
_____ Weather _____
Remarks _____
_____
_____
_____

Tuesday _____
Hrs. Sleeping _____ Weight _____ Pulse/Waking _____ Rising ____ Diff _____
Nutrition _____
_____

Distance ridden today _____ Workout type _____
Course _____
_____
_____ Weather _____
Remarks _____
_____
_____
_____

Wednesday _____
Hrs. Sleeping _____ Weight _____ Pulse/Waking _____ Rising ____ Diff _____
Nutrition _____
_____

Distance ridden today _____ Workout type _____
Course _____
_____
_____ Weather _____
Remarks _____
_____
_____
_____

Thursday _____

Hrs. Sleeping _____ Weight _____ Pulse/Waking _____ Rising _____ Diff _____

Nutrition _____

_____

Distance ridden today _____ Workout type _____

Course _____

_____

_____ Weather _____

Remarks _____

_____

_____

_____

Friday _____

Hrs. Sleeping _____ Weight _____ Pulse/Waking _____ Rising _____ Diff _____

Nutrition _____

_____

Distance ridden today _____ Workout type _____

Course _____

_____

_____ Weather _____

Remarks _____

_____

_____

_____

Saturday _____

Hrs. Sleeping _____ Weight _____ Pulse/Waking _____ Rising _____ Diff _____

Nutrition _____

_____

Distance ridden today _____ Workout type _____

Course _____

_____

_____ Weather _____

Remarks _____

_____

_____

_____

Sunday _____

Hrs. Sleeping _____ Weight _____ Pulse/Waking _____ Rising _____ Diff _____

Nutrition _____

_____

Distance ridden today _____ Workout type _____

Course _____

_____

_____ Weather _____

Remarks _____

_____

_____

_____

Race

Date _____ Time of Start _____ Event _____

Distance _____ Category ridden _____

Placing _____ Time _____

Competition _____

_____

Weather _____

Equipment _____

_____

Remarks _____

_____

_____

Weekly Summary

Distance this week _____

Mechanical notes _____

_____

_____

_____

Remarks _____

_____

_____

_____

_____

_____

Week of _____

Monday _____
Hrs. Sleeping _____ Weight _____ Pulse/Waking _____ Rising _____ Diff _____
Nutrition _____
_____

Distance ridden today _____ Workout type _____
Course _____
_____
_____ Weather _____
Remarks _____
_____
_____
_____

Tuesday _____
Hrs. Sleeping _____ Weight _____ Pulse/Waking _____ Rising _____ Diff _____
Nutrition _____
_____

Distance ridden today _____ Workout type _____
Course _____
_____
_____ Weather _____
Remarks _____
_____
_____
_____

Wednesday _____
Hrs. Sleeping _____ Weight _____ Pulse/Waking _____ Rising _____ Diff _____
Nutrition _____
_____

Distance ridden today _____ Workout type _____
Course _____
_____
_____ Weather _____
Remarks _____
_____
_____
_____

Thursday _____

Hrs. Sleeping _____ Weight _____ Pulse/Waking _____ Rising _____ Diff _____

Nutrition _____

_____

Distance ridden today _____ Workout type _____

Course _____

_____

_____ Weather _____

Remarks _____

_____

_____

_____

Friday _____

Hrs. Sleeping _____ Weight _____ Pulse/Waking _____ Rising _____ Diff _____

Nutrition _____

_____

Distance ridden today _____ Workout type _____

Course _____

_____

_____ Weather _____

Remarks _____

_____

_____

_____

Saturday _____

Hrs. Sleeping _____ Weight _____ Pulse/Waking _____ Rising _____ Diff _____

Nutrition _____

_____

Distance ridden today _____ Workout type _____

Course _____

_____

_____ Weather _____

Remarks _____

_____

_____

_____

Sunday _____

Hrs. Sleeping _____ Weight _____ Pulse/Waking _____ Rising _____ Diff _____

Nutrition _____

_____

Distance ridden today _____ Workout type _____

Course _____

_____

_____ Weather _____

Remarks _____

_____

_____

_____

Race

Date _____ Time of Start _____ Event _____

Distance _____ Category ridden _____

Placing _____ Time _____

Competition _____

_____

Weather _____

Equipment _____

_____

Remarks _____

_____

_____

Weekly Summary

Distance this week _____

Mechanical notes _____

_____

_____

_____

Remarks _____

_____

_____

_____

_____

_____

Week of _____

Monday _____
Hrs. Sleeping _____ Weight _____ Pulse/Waking _____ Rising _____ Diff _____
Nutrition _____
_____
Distance ridden today _____ Workout type _____
Course _____
_____
_____ Weather _____
Remarks _____
_____
_____
_____

Tuesday _____
Hrs. Sleeping _____ Weight _____ Pulse/Waking _____ Rising _____ Diff _____
Nutrition _____
_____
Distance ridden today _____ Workout type _____
Course _____
_____
_____ Weather _____
Remarks _____
_____
_____
_____

Wednesday _____
Hrs. Sleeping _____ Weight _____ Pulse/Waking _____ Rising _____ Diff _____
Nutrition _____
_____
Distance ridden today _____ Workout type _____
Course _____
_____
_____ Weather _____
Remarks _____
_____
_____
_____

Thursday _____

Hrs. Sleeping _____ Weight _____ Pulse/Waking _____ Rising _____ Diff _____

Nutrition _____

_____

Distance ridden today _____ Workout type _____

Course _____

_____

_____ Weather _____

Remarks _____

_____

_____

_____

Friday _____

Hrs. Sleeping _____ Weight _____ Pulse/Waking _____ Rising _____ Diff _____

Nutrition _____

_____

Distance ridden today _____ Workout type _____

Course _____

_____

_____ Weather _____

Remarks _____

_____

_____

_____

*'He told me that if I kept my legs warm
in cold weather and turned low gears,
I wouldn't have knee touble.
So I did, and I haven't.'*

Saturday _____

Hrs. Sleeping _____ Weight _____ Pulse/Waking _____ Rising _____ Diff _____

Nutrition _____

_____

Distance ridden today _____ Workout type _____

Course _____

_____

_____ Weather _____

Remarks _____

_____

_____

_____

1993 Dole criterium in Visalia, California.

Sunday _____

Hrs. Sleeping _____ Weight _____ Pulse/Waking _____ Rising _____ Diff _____

Nutrition _____

_____

Distance ridden today _____ Workout type _____

Course _____

_____

_____ Weather _____

Remarks _____

_____

_____

_____

Race

Date _____ Time of Start _____ Event _____

Distance _____ Category ridden _____

Placing _____ Time _____

Competition _____

_____

Weather _____

Equipment _____

_____

Remarks _____

_____

_____

Weekly Summary

Distance this week _____

Mechanical notes _____

_____

_____

_____

Remarks _____

_____

_____

_____

_____

Week of _____

Monday _____

Hrs. Sleeping _____ Weight _____ Pulse/Waking _____ Rising _____ Diff _____

Nutrition _____
_____

Distance ridden today _____ Workout type _____

Course _____
_____
_____ Weather _____

Remarks _____
_____
_____
_____

Tuesday

Hrs. Sleeping _____ Weight _____ Pulse/Waking _____ Rising _____ Diff _____

Nutrition _____
_____

Distance ridden today _____ Workout type _____

Course _____
_____
_____ Weather _____

Remarks _____
_____
_____
_____

Wednesday _____

Hrs. Sleeping _____ Weight _____ Pulse/Waking _____ Rising _____ Diff _____

Nutrition _____
_____

Distance ridden today _____ Workout type _____

Course _____
_____
_____ Weather _____

Remarks _____
_____
_____
_____

Thursday _____

Hrs. Sleeping _____ Weight _____ Pulse/Waking _____ Rising _____ Diff _____

Nutrition _____

_____

Distance ridden today _____ Workout type _____

Course _____

_____

_____ Weather _____

Remarks _____

_____

_____

_____

Friday _____

Hrs. Sleeping _____ Weight _____ Pulse/Waking _____ Rising _____ Diff _____

Nutrition _____

_____

Distance ridden today _____ Workout type _____

Course _____

_____

_____ Weather _____

Remarks _____

_____

_____

_____

Saturday _____

Hrs. Sleeping _____ Weight _____ Pulse/Waking _____ Rising _____ Diff _____

Nutrition _____

_____

Distance ridden today _____ Workout type _____

Course _____

_____

_____ Weather _____

Remarks _____

_____

_____

Sunday _____

Hrs. Sleeping _____ Weight _____ Pulse/Waking _____ Rising _____ Diff _____

Nutrition _____

_____

Distance ridden today _____ Workout type _____

Course _____

_____

_____ Weather _____

Remarks _____

_____

_____

_____

Race

Date _____ Time of Start _____ Event _____

Distance _____ Category ridden _____

Placing _____ Time _____

Competition _____

_____

Weather _____

Equipment _____

_____

Remarks _____

_____

_____

Weekly Summary

Distance this week _____

Mechanical notes _____

_____

_____

_____

Remarks _____

_____

_____

_____

_____

_____

Week of _____

Monday _____

Hrs. Sleeping _____ Weight _____ Pulse/Waking _____ Rising _____ Diff _____

Nutrition _____

_____

Distance ridden today _____ Workout type _____

Course _____

_____

_____ Weather _____

Remarks _____

_____

_____

_____

Tuesday _____

Hrs. Sleeping _____ Weight _____ Pulse/Waking _____ Rising _____ Diff _____

Nutrition _____

_____

Distance ridden today _____ Workout type _____

Course _____

_____

_____ Weather _____

Remarks _____

_____

_____

_____

Wednesday _____

Hrs. Sleeping _____ Weight _____ Pulse/Waking _____ Rising _____ Diff _____

Nutrition _____

_____

Distance ridden today _____ Workout type _____

Course _____

_____

_____ Weather _____

Remarks _____

_____

_____

_____

Thursday _____

Hrs. Sleeping _____ Weight _____ Pulse/Waking _____ Rising _____ Diff _____

Nutrition _____

_____

Distance ridden today _____ Workout type _____

Course _____

_____

_____ Weather _____

Remarks _____

_____

_____

_____

Friday _____

Hrs. Sleeping _____ Weight _____ Pulse/Waking _____ Rising _____ Diff _____

Nutrition _____

_____

Distance ridden today _____ Workout type _____

Course _____

_____

_____ Weather _____

Remarks _____

_____

_____

_____

Saturday _____

Hrs. Sleeping _____ Weight _____ Pulse/Waking _____ Rising _____ Diff _____

Nutrition _____

_____

Distance ridden today _____ Workout type _____

Course _____

_____

_____ Weather _____

Remarks _____

_____

_____

_____

Sunday _____

Hrs. Sleeping _____ Weight _____ Pulse/Waking _____ Rising _____ Diff _____

Nutrition _____

_____

Distance ridden today _____ Workout type _____

Course _____

_____

_____ Weather _____

Remarks _____

_____

_____

_____

Race

Date _____ Time of Start _____ Event _____

Distance _____ Category ridden _____

Placing _____ Time _____

Competition _____

_____

Weather _____

Equipment _____

_____

Remarks _____

_____

_____

Weekly Summary

Distance this week _____

Mechanical notes _____

_____

_____

_____

Remarks _____

_____

_____

_____

_____

_____

Monthly summary for ―――――――――――――――

Week of _____ Distance ridden_____

Week of _____ Distance ridden_____

Week of _____ Distance ridden_____

Week of _____ Distance ridden_____

Week of _____ Distance ridden_____

Total for month_____

Notes _____

_____

_____

_____

_____

_____

_____

_____

_____

_____

_____

_____

_____

_____

_____

_____

_____

_____

_____

_____

_____

Monthly summary for ———————————————————

Week of _____   Distance ridden_____

Week of _____   Distance ridden_____

Week of _____   Distance ridden_____

Week of _____   Distance ridden_____

Week of _____   Distance ridden_____

Total for month_____

Notes _____

_____

_____

_____

_____

_____

_____

_____

_____

_____

_____

_____

_____

_____

_____

_____

_____

_____

_____

_____

Monthly summary for ——————————————

Week of _____ Distance ridden_____

Week of _____ Distance ridden_____

Week of _____ Distance ridden_____

Week of _____ Distance ridden_____

Week of _____ Distance ridden_____

Total for month_____

Notes _____

_____

_____

_____

_____

_____

_____

_____

_____

_____

_____

_____

_____

_____

_____

_____

_____

_____

_____

Monthly summary for _____

Week of _____ Distance ridden_____

Week of _____ Distance ridden_____

Week of _____ Distance ridden_____

Week of _____ Distance ridden_____

Week of _____ Distance ridden_____

Total for month_____

Notes _____

_____

_____

_____

_____

_____

_____

_____

_____

_____

_____

_____

_____

_____

_____

_____

_____

_____

_____

_____

_____

_____

Monthly summary for _____

Week of _____ Distance ridden_____

Week of _____ Distance ridden_____

Week of _____ Distance ridden_____

Week of _____ Distance ridden_____

Week of _____ Distance ridden_____

Total for month_____

Notes _____

_____
_____
_____
_____
_____
_____
_____
_____
_____
_____
_____
_____
_____
_____
_____
_____
_____
_____
_____
_____
_____
_____

Monthly summary for _____

Week of _____ Distance ridden_____

Week of _____ Distance ridden_____

Week of _____ Distance ridden_____

Week of _____ Distance ridden_____

Week of _____ Distance ridden_____

Total for month_____

Notes _____

_____

_____

_____

_____

_____

_____

_____

_____

_____

_____

_____

_____

_____

_____

_____

_____

_____

_____

_____

_____

Monthly summary for ———————————————————

Week of _____ Distance ridden_____

Week of _____ Distance ridden_____

Week of _____ Distance ridden_____

Week of _____ Distance ridden_____

Week of _____ Distance ridden_____

Total for month_____

Notes _____

_____

_____

_____

_____

_____

_____

_____

_____

_____

_____

_____

_____

_____

_____

_____

_____

_____

_____

Monthly summary for _____

Week of _____   Distance ridden_____

Week of _____   Distance ridden_____

Week of _____   Distance ridden_____

Week of _____   Distance ridden_____

Week of _____   Distance ridden_____

                                      Total for month_____

Notes _____

_____

_____

_____

_____

_____

_____

_____

_____

_____

_____

_____

_____

_____

_____

_____

_____

_____

_____

_____

_____

_____

Monthly summary for ⸺⸺⸺⸺⸺

Week of ⸺⸺⸺⸺⸺   Distance ridden⸺⸺⸺

Week of ⸺⸺⸺⸺⸺   Distance ridden⸺⸺⸺

Week of ⸺⸺⸺⸺⸺   Distance ridden⸺⸺⸺

Week of ⸺⸺⸺⸺⸺   Distance ridden⸺⸺⸺

Week of ⸺⸺⸺⸺⸺   Distance ridden⸺⸺⸺

Total for month⸺⸺⸺

Notes ⸺⸺⸺⸺⸺⸺⸺⸺⸺⸺⸺⸺⸺

⸺⸺⸺⸺⸺⸺⸺⸺⸺⸺⸺⸺⸺⸺⸺⸺⸺

⸺⸺⸺⸺⸺⸺⸺⸺⸺⸺⸺⸺⸺⸺⸺⸺⸺

⸺⸺⸺⸺⸺⸺⸺⸺⸺⸺⸺⸺⸺⸺⸺⸺⸺

⸺⸺⸺⸺⸺⸺⸺⸺⸺⸺⸺⸺⸺⸺⸺⸺⸺

⸺⸺⸺⸺⸺⸺⸺⸺⸺⸺⸺⸺⸺⸺⸺⸺⸺

⸺⸺⸺⸺⸺⸺⸺⸺⸺⸺⸺⸺⸺⸺⸺⸺⸺

⸺⸺⸺⸺⸺⸺⸺⸺⸺⸺⸺⸺⸺⸺⸺⸺⸺

⸺⸺⸺⸺⸺⸺⸺⸺⸺⸺⸺⸺⸺⸺⸺⸺⸺

⸺⸺⸺⸺⸺⸺⸺⸺⸺⸺⸺⸺⸺⸺⸺⸺⸺

⸺⸺⸺⸺⸺⸺⸺⸺⸺⸺⸺⸺⸺⸺⸺⸺⸺

⸺⸺⸺⸺⸺⸺⸺⸺⸺⸺⸺⸺⸺⸺⸺⸺⸺

⸺⸺⸺⸺⸺⸺⸺⸺⸺⸺⸺⸺⸺⸺⸺⸺⸺

⸺⸺⸺⸺⸺⸺⸺⸺⸺⸺⸺⸺⸺⸺⸺⸺⸺

⸺⸺⸺⸺⸺⸺⸺⸺⸺⸺⸺⸺⸺⸺⸺⸺⸺

⸺⸺⸺⸺⸺⸺⸺⸺⸺⸺⸺⸺⸺⸺⸺⸺⸺

⸺⸺⸺⸺⸺⸺⸺⸺⸺⸺⸺⸺⸺⸺⸺⸺⸺

⸺⸺⸺⸺⸺⸺⸺⸺⸺⸺⸺⸺⸺⸺⸺⸺⸺

⸺⸺⸺⸺⸺⸺⸺⸺⸺⸺⸺⸺⸺⸺⸺⸺⸺

Monthly summary for ―――――――――――――――――

Week of _____ Distance ridden_____

Week of _____ Distance ridden_____

Week of _____ Distance ridden_____

Week of _____ Distance ridden_____

Week of _____ Distance ridden_____

Total for month_____

Notes _____

_____

_____

_____

_____

_____

_____

_____

_____

_____

_____

_____

_____

_____

_____

_____

_____

_____

_____

_____

_____

Monthly summary for ————————————

Week of _____ Distance ridden_____

Week of _____ Distance ridden_____

Week of _____ Distance ridden_____

Week of _____ Distance ridden_____

Week of _____ Distance ridden_____

Total for month_____

Notes _____

_____

_____

_____

_____

_____

_____

_____

_____

_____

_____

_____

_____

_____

_____

_____

_____

_____

_____

_____

_____

Monthly summary for ———————————————————

Week of _____ Distance ridden_____

Week of _____ Distance ridden_____

Week of _____ Distance ridden_____

Week of _____ Distance ridden_____

Week of _____ Distance ridden_____

Total for month_____

Notes _____

_____

_____

_____

_____

_____

_____

_____

_____

_____

_____

_____

_____

_____

_____

_____

_____

_____

_____

_____

_____